Adrenaline Junkie

Adventures of a Cajun Test Pilot

By Berchman Richard

To Paul

Enjoy the Rush !

Berchman Richard

Adrenaline Junkie
Adventures of a Cajun Test Pilot

By: Berchman Richard

Edited by Pam Eddings

Cover design by Cindy Moore

For information on ordering books by Berchman Richard, please communicate by email to **berchmanr@aol.com.**

FOLLOW ME on FACEBOOK: Berchman Richard

Dedication

This book is dedicated to the memory of my departed son, John Bernard Richard, who left us too soon.

I know God will be happy to have such a good cook in Heaven.

In addition, I wish to honor the memory of my uncle Bernard and the crew of his B-25 which were lost on a mission over the Aleutians during WWII. He's the second one on the right, the top turret gunner.

Table of Contents

Part I
The Little Cajun

The Opening

The sun was just rising over east Burbank as I drove my Alfa Romeo through the gates of the Lockheed California plant. After parking the car, I walked up to a waiting DC-3 on the ramp, its engines slowly ticking over. Climbing aboard, I walked up the aisle to the cockpit where I greeted the pilots. Then I sat down and awaited the takeoff for the short flight to the Lockheed flight test facility on the California coast. Waiting for me there was a state-of-the-art compound helicopter, the most advanced helicopter in the world, and I would be flying it later in the day. I was eagerly looking forward to climbing into the cockpit, starting the powerful GE jet engine, and getting airborne. I loved to fly, and it all began many years ago in Central Louisiana.

I am a small Cajun man, born in south Louisiana to a working-class family. I completed college at a local college, McNeese State, by working nights at the local oil refinery as a helper, boilermaker, welder, insulator, and even a guard while carrying a full class load during the day. My goal was to get a degree so I could enter the armed services as an officer and qualify for flight school.

This is a story of the many adventures in my life. My appearance was deceiving, since I was neither tall, handsome, wealthy, or any of the other attributes that are normally associated with men of adventure. I was a small, quiet, unassuming man, who led a life that most men would envy. My name is Berchman Richard, the little Cajun test pilot.

During my lifetime, in addition to later becoming a test pilot at Lockheed California Company, I also became a racing driver in both production cars, and formula cars. Along the way, I also became interested in sailing, owning a Columbia 26, which I sailed many times to Catalina Island, and eventually was part of the crew on a world-famous racing boat called SHOCKWAVE.

After my flying career, I became a business man, manufacturing my own patented bike rack for city buses, and the coin-operating snow ski locking racks found on 200 ski resorts around the country.

I started a company called Malibu Pipe Line which manufactured and sold patio furniture; later the company expanded to include Pacific Coast Patio and spas. Many of my customers were movie stars who lived along the Malibu coast.

After returning to my home state of Louisiana, I became involved in the media business, first in radio, and later as the General Manager of the local FOX television station. My love of the television business led me, along with some good motorcycling friends, to develop a television series titled *Hog Heaven, The TV Show.*

Sit back and enjoy my adventurous stories in the following pages.

Racing team at Mansfield, Louisiana. My father, my crew chief, Max Adams, the mechanic, me in the car, wife Marilyn beside me.

A Little Background Music Please

First, a little background on the little Cajun. There is nothing in the early years that foretold of the adventures to follow. But my upbringing by a wonderful Cajun couple instilled in me the love of life to pursue those experiences.

I was born in Lake Charles, Louisiana and spent my early years in my mother's hometown of Kinder, Louisiana. Kinder was dominated by my Grandfather, Willis Lormand. He was without a doubt the patriarch of the family. He and his wife, Ellen, were the social center of our world. Pa and Ma, as they were called by us, had four daughters, Lilly, Ethel, Wanda, and my mother, Virginia. Both sides of their family were very large French Acadian families. The Nevils and the Lormands both had about 12 to 13 children. They were not wealthy in terms of money even though Pa owned the local hardware store and had been Mayor at one point, but they lived and ate well. I inherited a sense of adventure from them since Pa, Ma, and the four girls all traveled to California in the 1920's over unpaved roads. Sometimes they had to wait for hours or days for repairs to be made to roads or bridges. My mother told how much the girls enjoyed these delays since Pa was a natural salesman and had stocked their auto with different goods that he sold to other stranded motorists. As a result, all the motorists would flock to their auto to trade and visit, and the girls became the center of attention.

Our immediate family had big gatherings at my grandparents' home at least once a month. For the annual family gatherings, we met the rest of our kin at the family camp on the bank of the Calcasieu River at Nevils Bluff.

Talk about food! At the camp, they would put together two picnic tables just for the food. We had to eat outside since there was no room inside. All the women would bring their favorite dish, and you had to sample them all if you didn't want to slight anyone. Needless to say, you did not stop eating until you could not eat another bite. It was all so delicious, and of course I took it all for granted. After all, didn't everyone eat that well? It wasn't until years later when I went into the Army that I found out how well I had been eating all those years.

On most weekends, the husbands of the four daughters would arrive at the end of Friday evenings, then they would run fishing lines all night for the meal on Saturday. After catching enough fish, they would spend the rest of the night talking together while they cleaned the fish and drank beer. The next morning, all the women and children would arrive to find a big pile of fish cleaned and ready to be cooked, which they proceeded to do while the menfolk caught up on their sleep. Then everyone gathered around the big table to eat and talk until dark. It was a very special time to be growing up.

I attended and graduated from LaGrange High School, which at that time was the poor boys school. My father, JB, as everyone called him, worked as a clerk in the maintenance department at the Cities Service Oil Refinery located across the lake. My mother, Virginia, never worked outside our home. It would have been an insult to my father if she would have. Women did not work in those days; the men worked, and the women took care of the home and children. My mother would wake me up in the morning with a fresh cup of hot coffee, and the smell of bacon and eggs coming from the kitchen. I was not allowed to eat until my room was straight and the bed made. Mother also prepared a good lunch for me to bring to school. There were no school buses in those days; I either walked or rode my bike to school. I was not a particularly good student, but I enjoyed the simple life I was leading.

The Cajun Zip line

Some people would have you believe that we Cajuns tend to be a little backwards. But it *ain't*[1] necessarily so. A real popular sport that is now going around is the ZIP LINE where a cable is strung between two high points, and people slide down the cable, hanging on to a handle attached to a wheel on the line. People get all excited about this new way to taste a little adventure.

Well, we Cajuns had *us* a zip line a long time ago. Let me tell you about it, *shă*.

When I was growing up, we spent almost every weekend at the family camp on the Calcasieu River. The camp had been built by my grandfather's four sons-in-law, and we passed some good times there. It was built on a bluff overlooking the river below, with a beautiful white sand bar on the other side of the fast-flowing river. The camp was just outside the little community of Indian Village where my grandmother had grown up. She told the story of her mother baking two pies, and leaving them on the window sill to cool. While sitting there, the Indians would come up and take one of the pies. They never took both, just the one.

The bluff, called Nevils Bluff, was high over the river and had a tall tree standing right on the edge. The sons-in-law stretched a cable from the top of the tree on the edge of the bluff all the way across the river and anchored it to a tree on the sandbar on the other side. Over the cable, they slipped a piece of pipe about 5-6 inches long. We would climb up the tree, take hold of the piece of pipe, walk out on the end of the limb, and launch our self into the air, holding tightly onto that piece of pipe.

The pipe slid down the cable with us holding on for dear life; there were no safety nets or anything, just hanging by our hands as we slid across the river below. At the mid-point, we were pretty high in the

---

[1] Some of the italicized words in this chapter are purposely added to demonstrate Cajun ways of expression.

air, and the river was too shallow to drop at that point. It was quite a thrill, and the guys all loved it. The women didn't; they thought it was foolish and risky and wanted it torn down. But the men resisted since every one of us wanted to experience it.

On the day I took a turn for the first time, I climbed up the tree, took hold of the piece of pipe, walked out on the limb, took a deep breath, and pushed away from the tree. It was exciting, and daring to be that high over the river. It was a rush, until the pipe stopped. I was too light; as a teenager, I was only about 120 pounds soaking wet and didn't have the weight to keep the pipe sliding down the cable. I stopped right at the highest point over the river, and there I hung. The women were really upset by then, and the men were all yelling solutions, none of which worked.

I started to hop the pipe to try and get it to slide. It only moved a few inches at a time, and I hung on tightly as I tried to work my way down to the sandbar. As I neared the bottom, I released the pipe and dropped down into the shallow water. I was a hero at this point, and enjoyed all the comments everyone was making.

So ended the zip line experiment. The women prevailed, and the cable was removed. But we had proven that we Cajuns *ain't* so dumb, *no*!

Paddling on the Calcasieu River with my dog and son, John.

The Lormand clan at the camp on Nevils Bluff. My wife, Marilyn and son, John are on far left. My dad is in white shirt, third from right. My mother, Virginia and sister, JoAnn are next to him.

The Early Days Of Sports Car Racing

My father was totally against me racing sports cars. While still in college, I planned on racing with my only automobile, my MG-A.

One day, however, I arrived home from school and prepared to go to my job at the oil refinery when I saw a beautiful chrome roll bar sitting in my garage. A driver in those days wasn't required to have a roll bar installed in his car, but this one was made to fit in my MG-A.

I went into the house to confront my father, and in a gruff voice his response was, "Well, if I couldn't convince you not to race, the only thing I could do was try to protect your fool head!"

So Dad became part of my racing team as team manager along with my mechanic, Max Adams, and my wife as the time keeper. Max was an excellent mechanic, plus he also drove an MG-A which he planned to race the following year. My wife would sit on top of my Dad's Chevy Nova station wagon and time the other competitors in my class. She was pretty good at pointing out the cars for which I should be watching. However, occasionally she would overlook a particular

car with which we were familiar, a car which had never been any competition in the past.

On one occasion, at another airport circuit in Louisiana, I shared the front row of the starting grid with a car that usually qualified in the rear of the grid. Imagine my surprise when at the drop of the starter's flag, that car took off and left me in his smoke! It was the same car, but a different driver, and he knew his business.

So that started the battle. I tried to get the inside line on the corners, but he always managed to move over just in time to block me, and I couldn't pull up alongside of him on the straightaways; he was just too fast. And so the race went, both of us driving all out to gain an advantage, but the positions never changed.

Finally I got to thinking, "Well, I can just coast and take second place, which is still pretty good considering the size of the field. Then I decided, "No, I didn't come here to finish second; I came to win!"

I started paying close attention to all his moves, watching his racing lines through the corners, point of braking, accelerations, his top speed on the straight, his shift points, and his attitude as he drove around the track. I quit trying to get by him. I just maintained my position, luring him to relax a little.

Then finally, on the last lap, on the last corner, I began to accelerate around the outside of him, and when he moved over to block me, I dove inside of him and slid through the corner, forcing him to the outside edge. Now a car length ahead of him and heading for the finish line, it became a drag race! I could hear his engine screaming above mine as he tried to retake the lead, but the car length I had on him was enough to get me past the finish line ahead of him. My pit crew was ecstatic when I pulled into the pits. It was a wonderful moment when I took my wife around the circuit holding the checkered flag.

It was a wonderful day, but it wasn't over. Later, as most of the other teams were leaving the track, my father asked me what it was like out there on the track. I told him to climb in, and I would take him for a lap. (The rules were a lot looser then.) He put on his seat belt, borrowed a helmet, and I took him around the track at a normal road speed lap. When we returned to the pit, he said that wasn't bad, not nearly what he had expected. I told him I was only driving at about 6/10s, not a real racing speed. That pace would have put me at the back of the pack. He said he wanted to see what it was really like, and wanted to go faster. We went out on the track again, and this time, I sped up to around 8/10s. That was enough to be competitive, but not a front runner, sliding around corners, shifting up through the gears while keeping the RPM's at maximum. When we finally pulled into the pits, I asked him what he thought now. His answer was, "that's enough." He never asked again.

When I left college for the Army, my dad continued with the Sports Car Club of America as an official at the local sports car races at courses in south Louisiana. Those racing days we shared were some of the best we ever had together. I still miss him.

Expanding Your Comfort Zone

Leading an exciting life has strict requirements. You find yourself in situations you haven't experienced before. Most of us go through life in a comfort zone, no real risks, taking no chances. But to really go for it, you must be willing to leave that comfort zone and enter into unknown areas which require real risks, and danger.

Taking risks can apply not only to sports, but also to other aspects of your life as well, including business, relationships, travel, and just going through life on a daily basis.

Following are several stories where I had to leave my comfort zone behind and take chances if I was going to really experience life.

Auto Racing Adventures

While attending college, I fell in love with sports cars, which were a new thing in the Deep South, and I became a race car driver on a very limited budget. At that time, you could earn money driving a race car because race proceeds were donated to charities which allowed racers to claim a tax deduction for every race.

It was a quiet Saturday morning, and I was sitting on my front porch when a good friend, Monte Hurley, drove up in a funny-looking little car. It was a convertible with a square grill painted green, with matching leather seats, a cut-down door, and wire wheels. Very exotic looking. Monte said it was an MG-TD, an English sports car, which was the rage. There was a race up in Mansfield, Louisiana the next day, and he offered to drive me there in his little car to watch it. The next morning, we set off on an adventure which eventually changed my life. I fell in love with the MG, and also found my sport as I watched the cars race around the airport track. I thought to himself, "I have finally found my sport!" The girls were impressed, but the small two-seater kept romance to a minimum.

During a trip to see a sports car race in Hammond, Louisiana with my bride-to-be, the engine started blowing black smoke and making loud noises. The end result was that I had to be towed back home behind my Grandfather's blue Cadillac, large fins and all. It was quite an embarrassing end to the weekend. And to the TD.

My Dad and I towed it to Houston, Texas and traded the TD in on a new MG-A. This car played a big role in my life. I took my honeymoon in it, and it became my first race car.

I had entered and won many different driving events and realized I was a naturally fast driver, outperforming drivers in fastest cars without a lot of effort. As a result, I decided to become a race car driver. I entered a sports car race being held in Mansfield, LA. He borrowed a crash helmet, pulled off the windshield, put some numbers on the side of the car, and drove to the race track. I even still had white sidewall street tires. As a beginner, I had to enter the novice race, and won it! In those days, if you performed well in the novice race, you were allowed to compete the next day in the feature race.

While practicing on the course, I realized the fast guys were much faster than I was, and I couldn't figure that out, especially since I considered myself a very fast driver. Determined to find out what they were doing that made them so fast, I tucked in behind one of the fast guys to follow him around the track, and see what he was doing. At 105 mph, we went through the high speed turn at the end of the straightaway with no problem. Next, was a hard, right-hand turn, which tightened up as you went through it. I watched the car to see his taillights flash, indicating he was braking. But they didn't come on, and I found myself going deeper into the corner than I had ever gone. Out of control, I finally straightened the car out and continued to the next corner, this time a 90-degree left-hand corner. Once again, I had to fight to keep the car under control as the experienced driver waited until the last minute to brake before turning. This happened over and over again until the lap was complete. I pulled into the pit and just sat there. My wife asked if I was okay, and I asked her to just leave me alone. I realized that to go really fast, I was going to have to push the limits to an edge I had never experienced and dig deep into my guts to drive a car at racing speeds. I was naturally fast, but racing against experienced drivers required a lot more than that. So, I learned to expand my comfort one and enter into a new dimension.

Flying Adventure

Another experience happened while flying an L-19 Bird-dog aircraft for the 101st Airborne on maneuvers called Swift Strike. While on an observation mission, I spotted some troops on the ground and decided to go down to identify them. I pulled up into a wingover, and dove in a steep dive to tree top level. I pulled up just over the top of the trees when my engine stopped. Although I went through all the emergency procedures, the engine refused to start. In front of me was an open field, with a dense forest area just beyond. To get it down, I had to make the open field in spite of my airspeed which would have carried me into the trees. I ran down all the flaps, (60 degrees) put the ship into a big sideslip, and killed off the airspeed before settling down into the soft, plowed ground. The ship came to an immediate stop, and went up onto its nose, breaking the aircraft in the middle and collapsing the wings.

Thankfully, I was unharmed, but my back seat passenger had a knot on his head. The plane was totaled, but we were okay. A helicopter came in to pick us up and return to base, but it hit some power lines, and it crashed also. As a result, a temporary halt was called for the exercise, and the pilots retired to the officers club at a nearby airbase.

The flight surgeon pronounced me okay, and I joined my fellow pilots, dancing at the club with the available women. As I was dancing with an attractive woman in a tight dress, it dawned on me that I could have been dead, never to experience dancing with a pretty woman again. Suddenly, I was overcome with a feeling of exhilaration at being alive, having come close to experiencing death, and the rush that followed. That's when I realized that to really experience life, sometimes you had to brush close to death.

Racing A Formula Car

It was my 50th birthday. As I began looking back at my life, I realized that one of the things I had enjoyed most was racing sports cars. I really missed that major adrenaline rush I would feel while driving fast on a race course. Then it also dawned on me that living in Sacramento, California at the time put me between the two best race courses on the west coast. Laguna Seca was down south in Monterey, and Sears Point was in Sonoma up north. I wasn't getting any younger, so if I was going to get back into a racing car, I had better do it now.

Next decision was what kind of car I could race with the budget I had available. As a young man, I raced in production cars which were set up for racing, but using pretty much stock components. In my case it was an MG-A. The only problem with production was rule changes. One year you could have a class winning automobile; then, when a new car appeared in your class, you now owned a non-competitive car. That happened to me when the Elva Courier was placed in FP to run against us only because it used the same engine as the MG. The problem with the Courier was its fiberglass construction, making it about 500 pounds lighter, which resulted in it being faster right out of the box.

So, a production car was out. That left either a sports-racer or formula car. Sports-racers were expensive, built strictly for racing, could not be driven on a street, and were very delicate as well as very fast. That left a formula car. A formula car is a single seat, open wheel race car like you see at an Indy car race. These are pure race cars. Nothing much but a frame, gas tank, engine, and suspension all covered by a thin fiberglass body. With no windshield, there was very little driver protection; there was a roll bar behind your head, and another behind the instrument panel, offering a little protection for your head in a roll-over. For the pure sensation of racing at speed, nothing beats a formula car. However, it is expensive.

Then I discovered a unique class, called Formula Vee. These rear engine cars made use of Volkswagen parts, brakes, suspension, and engine. And they never changed the rules. A good FV could be competitive for years. In the beginning, most were homemade, but that changed quickly as the class became more popular and competitive. They normally had the biggest race grids of any class at any event.

This car sounded a lot more like what I needed. I began my search and found one through a race car prep shop owned by Bob Cornish. At the beginning of a season, you would tow your car to Bob's shop, and the two of you would determine which races you wanted to enter that season. Then Bob would go through the car, making adjustments and repairs as needed, and deliver the car to the track, race-ready. He had a race car hauler and a tent set up to park the cars under the shade; in addition, he gave the drivers a place to hang out and get into their racing suits.

Bob was not only a superior mechanic; he was also an ex-Formula Vee champion, having been the west coast champion a couple of times. So, he also became my racing coach. He would walk me around a course, talking about how to properly go through each corner. Sometimes he would spray paint a circle on the course at the entrance to a turn and tell me he wanted my left front tire to go over that circle at 4500 RPM in third gear without braking. Instructions like that always pushed me to go faster than I thought I could.

The next step was driving school. You don't just show up in a race car at the track and start racing. It's too dangerous, especially for the other drivers. Two weekends of schooling were required before you were granted a competition driver's license.

The first weekend involved all classroom at a local college. The room was packed on the first day. Then the instructors began talking about driving really fast, not street racing fast, but road course racing fast. It was a completely different ball game. At one point the instructor told us, "This is not a stick and ball game; this is a blood sport, and people get killed doing this! If you can't afford to totally wreck your car with no insurance, you shouldn't be doing this."

By the start of the classroom session the next day, fully one half of the attendees had dropped out.

The following weekend, we reported to a race track with a race car properly equipped with roll bars, fire extinguishers, etc. The size of the class had been reduced by another 50%. First, we received a lecture about behavior at the track, both in the pits and on the course. Finally we got in our race car and with two or three other novices, followed an instructor around the course. After each lap, he drove a little faster until pretty soon, the fast boys were separating from the rest; before some of the drivers lost full control, he pulled us into the pits. There was more talk about fast driving since by now some of us were starting to understand it wasn't all about a heavy right foot.

The next day we finally got to take part in an actual race; even though it was only against fellow students, at least it was a real race on a real course with a real race car.

My sons, Brett and John, showed up with another friend to act as my pit crew. Brett introduced me to ear plugs. I had never worn ear plugs during all the loud environments in my past, including the Army, helicopters, race cars, and music. I asked him what they were for and he replied, "Just trying to save what little hearing you have left."

The race car I had purchased was called a Zink; although it was not the latest car, it was a good car for the school. It was a very popular model, but was considered a beginners car. That was okay, as I was a beginner at this point. The race began, and I was enjoying myself. I had even passed a few cars when I received a black flag as I went past the starters' box. A black flag means something is wrong with your car, and you must pull off into the pits. I pulled into the pits where my two boys were waiting for me; I had no idea what could be wrong since the engine sounded good, and the gauges looked okay. They stopped me and told me to kill the engine. I shut it off and sat there while they went to work behind my head. In a formula car, the roll bar goes up alongside your head so you can't turn your head sideways. You have to use your rear view mirrors to see behind you. Finally, they said to start it, then patted me on the head to indicate I could leave the pits.

When the race was over and I pulled back into our regular pit area, I asked them what had been the problem. They told me the engine cover had come loose and the whole thing was flopping up and down in the air steam as I went around the course. I was wondering why I couldn't go any faster, but I had the engine cover acting as a big wing break. They never let me forget it.

What is it like to drive a Formula car? It is very exciting, much more so than a production car. It is small, the engine is right behind your head, the seat is actually the gas tank, and the exhaust has no mufflers. If you're competitive, you're running the engine flat out so the roar right behind your head is very loud. The sides of the car are up against your shoulders, and you have to pull the steering wheel off to get in and out of the car. The FV had slick tires. Slick tires have no threads. They get their grip from the heat of the tire; the rubber is very soft and provides grip only when you get them hot and the rubber gets sticky. They have no holding power in the rain or cold.

One day I arrived early to practice before a race at Sears Point. By then I was driving a faster car called a Lynx. It was very slick, painted in gun-medal blue with a yellow nose and stripe running down the side. I was also qualifying in mid pack of about 30 cars, so I pretty fast. I always tried to get as much practice as I could, so I was always on the track as soon as our class was allowed. I took a few laps at a reduced speed to warm the tires up before really pushing it. Finally, I felt the tires were warm enough and put my foot down to begin a hot lap. I started to accelerate down the straight and through the left hander, which is turn 1. At that point, the course starts up the hill to turn 2, which is a 90% right-hander at the top of the hill. After making the turn, the road drops so you are rotating the car at the top of the hill.

I was now at racing speed heading for turn 2 and began to downshift to slow the car down for the turn. I turned the wheel to the right to turn the car, but nothing happened! The car continued straight as I slammed head-on into the wall. The nose of the car went up into the air as the car pivoted around the right rear tire, and dropped back down, pointed down the hill in the right direction. My adrenaline was working full time, and without a moment's thought, I dropped the car into a lower gear and accelerated back down the course. However, the front end was all messed up and bouncing around as I continued around the course to the pits. Bob took one look at the car and motioned me back to his truck. The tires were too cold, and had no grip. I was too eager to start driving fast, and that was the price I paid.

It took Bob the rest of the morning and into the afternoon to make the necessary repairs to the car, but he had me ready to enter the main event that afternoon. After the damage I had done to the car, I felt pretty good when I finished in the top ten.

Racing At Laguna Seca

This is a story about auto racing. When a driver arrives at a new race track, his goal is to reach a lap time which will make him competitive. This story follows a driver's first visit to one of the most famous race tracks in the country, Laguna Seca.

It was hot in the driver's suit, not from the sun, but from my own nervousness. It is hot work being a racing driver. The inside of the car is hot, the sun beating down on you in the cockpit is hot, the pace is hot, and right now I'm hot and not doing too well. I can't seem to bring my lap times down to a respectable level.

Bob Cornish, my driving instructor/race mechanic/friend knows how to get around race courses, and right now we're discussing what I have to do to improve my lap times. This is my first time at the famous Laguna Seca raceway near Monterey, California. This is the track where, many years ago, I had watched my hero, Sterling Moss, driving an awful pea green Lotus, come out of turn 7 shading his eyes from the afternoon sun with one hand, steering around the course with the other, all while leading the race. He had made it all look so easy. I was a young infantry officer stationed at Ft. Ord, and as I watched him, I hoped that someday I could drive around this beautiful twisting course with its famous corkscrew turn.

Well, many years later, the dream has come true. I had a beautiful race car, a Lynx Formula Vee, built and prepared by Cornish, and painted yellow and gray, the colors of the Confederate cavalry. But it was not easy, it was then a very high-speed course, with few slow turns, most of which were taken flat out. My speeds were not high at this point. As a matter of fact, I was in the 1:27 bracket, well off the pace. This was not unusual as I normally do better in the race even if it takes me a little longer than all the much younger drivers to get up to speed.

Bob and I were discussing my techniques in each of the corners. "Are you taking turn 1 flat out?" he asked. I nodded yes. "How about turn

2?" Again I nodded yes. Looking at me intensely, he asked the question I didn't want to hear. "Well, what about turn 3?" I answered somewhat sheepishly, "I back off, and sometimes I tap the brake a little if it seems my entrance speed is too high." "Berch," he said, you've got to take turn 3 flat out, it's an important turn. You need the speed coming out of it for the uphill climb to turn 4!" Turn 3 was a high speed left-hander with a slight dip in the middle right at the apex. It had lots of wide space on each side, but with deep, soft sand on the left side which would effectively stop the car. Then you're stuck until a tow truck can come and pull you out. It was marked by lots of black tire strips demonstrating how other drivers had foolishly (or bravely) gone in faster than they could handle.

"Bob" I said, "that's a real fast corner, I don't see how I can go around it flat out, I'm squirrelly enough as it is now. It frightens me a little already." With that intense look, Bob said, "Berch, you want to do a 1:23, you take turn 3 flat out." I knew that was the end of the subject; you either did it, or you had to accept the slow time. And of course a true race driver did not accept slow times; that is not what being a race driver is all about. It's about taking risks, chances, finding the car's limits, and pushing your own limits.

Once again I climbed into the cockpit, settled into my harness, and tried to mentally prepare myself to go through turn 3 flat out. The first two laps were just to get back into the rhythm of the circuit. That's something most people don't realize about race driving. It's not just all balls and going fast. You have to have an intimate relationship with the road, know its bumps, the curves, the dips, where to go fast, and where to go slow. The shifting, of course, is like dancing to the music, except the music is the sound of a race engine screaming in your ear, your score the tachometer registering your performance, and you're judged by the stopwatch.

Now I'm ready. I feel like I'm back up to speed. Turn 1 is taken flat out with no problem. Turn 2 is almost flat out, and turn 3 is approaching rapidly. I'm determined to keep my right foot planted on the floor. I remember a story about the great Canadian driver,

Gilles Villeneuve, when he first went to drive for Ferrari. He and the driver from Argentina, Carlos Reutemann, were lapping the test track, and Carlos was faster than Gilles. Now Carlos was older, and in Gilles' mind, that made him slower. Yet here, he was faster. He asked Carlos what he was doing, and Carlos pointed out a particular corner and said that he was taking it flat out. Gillles was shocked; he felt he could not take that corner flat out, and if he couldn't, how could Carlos? Yet Carlos was doing it, and to be a top ranked Formula 1 driver, Gilles knew that he most do it also. Yet, every time Gilles approached that corner, he lifted his right foot. He felt if he did not, he would crash. Finally, determined, as he once again came into that corner, he crossed his left foot over and put it over his right foot on the accelerator, then locked his left knee so that even if he tried, he would not be able to lift. With fear in his throat, prepared for the crash he knew would follow, he entered the turn flat out. He went through it, wildly, without crashing, and he equaled the lap time of Carlos.

Well, I wasn't going to get that dramatic, but I was determined. I kept my foot planted as I entered the turn. The car went through the apex at a speed that amazed me. But now I was unwinding the steering wheel as the car slid towards the outside of the turn. Right off the course, the car had a mind of its own, trying to get away from me. I held on, and eased her back onto the track. That overwhelming fear was now gone. I had gone through the corner flat out and survived. Now, all I had to do was develop a technique to keep all four wheels on the track instead of sliding off. Back up to speed again, I was preparing for the next lap and my duel with corner 3.

Here we go again, turn 3 is out there waiting for me as I drive through the course. But now, I am ready and enter the corner flat out, foot planted. Again, the speed through the apex is not quite as intimidating as before. The car is still fighting me though, and drifts to the outside edge, where the right two wheels drop off the road. But I maintain control, and slowly bring it back. That wasn't too bad, and is actually acceptable if I don't let my speed drop too much. Once again, around I go, eagerly anticipating my next confrontation with my nemesis.

Into the turn, flat out, confident, and this time only the right rear slides off the pavement. But it's tricky and must be eased very carefully back where it belongs to avoid catching the edge which would cause me to skid across the track backwards and maybe tangle with a couple of other Vees coming through the corner. Now I've got it; that turn is mine, and once again the approach is made. The car slides towards the edge, but stops just where it should be, with the two outside wheels right on the edge of the racetrack. I've done it.

One more lap to be sure, and then I slow down and pull into the pits where Bob is waiting with that telltale stop watch in his hand. As I kill the engine, he leans over, and before I ask, he says "You did it, you did a 1:23!"

I wish I could say that was a new lap record, or even the fastest time of the day. But in fact, I was still off the pace of the front runners. Yet, for a 51-year-old race driver, driving for the first time on the challenging Laguna Seca race course, that was a good time.

The Crash At Sears Point Raceway

There are certain races that are open to specific people by invitation only. One of those was the Pacific Coast Road Racing Championships. To be selected, you have to finish in the top 50% of your racing car class in previous races for that season. That meant that the top racers on the west coast, from California to Washington would be competing.

When you're racing, you get used to the other racers you're competing against. You know how close together you can run with someone, how deep they will go into a corner, what kind of speed they normally carry, that sort of thing. In a race like the Pacific Coast Championship, you're racing against guys you've never seen before, so there is a great unknown factor going up against them.

I had heard rumors of some of them driving like wild men, going a little too far into corners, or driving over their heads, so we were all a little careful getting too close to some of these guys.

But the point was, I was invited. It was with a feeling of pride that I sewed that Pacific Coast patch on my driving suit. It meant that I was among the fastest Formula Vee drivers on the west coast, someone to be reckoned with even at my age. There were only 2 of us drivers who were 50 years old. Most were in their 30's and some even in their 20's, but the old man was still fast.

It turned out to be a beautiful day at Sears Point in Sonoma, California when I arrived at the track. Bob Cornish was there with the tent all set up, the car all polished and ready to race. My Formula Vee was a Lynx; I had it painted in Confederate cavalry colors, gun metal blue with a yellow nose and stripe running down the side. It was a pretty car, and fast.

I climbed into my driver's suit after attending the drivers meeting, and Bob gave me the go-ahead to get in. I stepped into the seat, then slid myself down under the dash, buckled into my harness, and put the steering wheel back in place. Bob adjusted my rear view mirrors so that I could keep track of cars behind me to keep them from passing while trying to pass the cars in front of me.

Finally we got the word to proceed to the pre-grid where the cars are lined up according to their qualifying speed. I was in the middle of the pack of about 30 cars. Not a front runner, but a respectable position. Then you sit there, waiting, reviewing the track in your mind, all the corners, braking points, shifts required, potential places to make a pass, or be passed. It's like watching a movie in your head of going around the course. That's why practice before a race is so important, to get that movie in your head so you can react instinctively.

Now the cars are moving onto the track, remaining in your designated place relative to the other cars, twisting the wheel left and right. There are a couple of reasons that drivers do this. One is to put heat in the tires. We were running Hoover slicks, which meant they had no tread, and they generated grip only when hot, so you twisted the wheel back and forth to get some heat before the start of the race, otherwise you couldn't go too fast.

The second reason was it helped the drivers get rid of their nerves, calm down, and get into the zone. It worked for me; by the time we had completed two warm-up laps, both my tires and I were ready to race.

Coming through the final turn onto the straight-away, the flag dropped, and the race was on. Everyone was jockeying for position as we ran through turn one and up the hill to turn 2. Going through turn 2, a right-handed at the top of the hill, I noticed a couple of cars tangled up on the right side of the course. That meant I had just gained two positions. The competition was fierce.

Down the hill through turn 3 and flying through air as you entered the carousel, and a couple of more cars were on the sidelines. I'm moving up the grid and keeping a fast pace. As I turn right onto the straight-away leading to the "S" curves, I notice a strange car pulling up close behind me. It's not a car I'm familiar with, which means it's a driver I need to watch for. We got thru the series of "S" curves which lead to the final high speed turn behind the tower, which is normally a pretty tricky turn since you maintain your speed all the way through it. Just as we were entering it, the car behind me dives inside of me trying to take the inside line and pass me. It is an unusual move, and not one that most drivers would take because of the speed and leading up to one of the slowest corners on the track. It surprises me; I glance sideways which takes away my concentration, and the rear end of my car slides out. I begin a high speed spin and slam into the tire wall backwards, hard. My rear wheels are up on top of the tire wall, and my front tires are on the race course as the car comes to a stop. The marshals run out waving yellow flags and help me climb out of my car.

They escort me to the medical station for a checkup where the doctors check me out. I don't seem to have any serious injuries, so they release me. After the race, my car is towed over to Bob's truck. It's pretty torn up, the rear end all messed up with the impact. It's the final race of the year, so Bob loads it into his truck to return to his shop for repairs. It was a pretty sad ending for what was a good season.

I return home and go back to work on Monday. But something isn't right. I have no strength in my right arm. I can hardly open my car door, and can't shift gears with it. When I place my left hand over my right forearm, it's very hot. My secretary tells me to get that checked out. My co-driver in Bob's stable is connected to the medical field, and she recommends I see a doctor in San Francisco. He checks me out and wants to perform an operation on my neck which means I will go thru life not being able to turn my head sideways anymore.

I say no to that, and finally I am recommended to a chiropractor. She does some tests, and says that when I impacted that wall, I pinched a nerve in my spine, and she can release the pressure with a few visits. She goes to work, and slowly I begin to regain the use of my right arm. However, both she and the doctor in San Francisco tell me that my racing days are over. I was lucky the only damage done was a pinched nerve. The impact I had could have damaged my neck muscles or even snapped my neck. Once before I ran straight into a wall at high speed and remember how it had hurt as my head was thrown forward while my body was restrained by my seat harness and I thought, "Wow, that hurt!"

For once I took someone's recommendation and decided at my age, it was time to hang up my helmet. Sadly, I had Bob sell my car and decided to look into another aspect of racing besides driving. My next adventure was to become a racing team manager and part owner of a team of Sports 2000 race cars in a series called the American Cities Racing League. But that's a whole other story.

Part II
Flying in the Army

Louisiana Flyers

Louisiana Flyers was a first class crop-dusting operation based at the local airport in Lake Charles, Louisiana. They flew WWII trainer bi-planes which were real popular called Stearmans. The original canvas covered fuselages had been re-covered in aluminum and painted green and white. They were very handsome birds. And they were flown by a group of very talented pilots, one of whom is the subject of this story, Rocky Taylor.

Rocky was a legend at the time. He didn't just work a field, he put on an air show. The farmers would schedule him far in advance, and show up with their entire families and friends to watch him work their fields. He was smooth, and used to show off when taxiing out to the airstrip by gunning the engine, lifting the tail wheel off the ground while standing still, and taxi out on just the two main landing gears. Their green and white ships, maintained in beautiful condition, were a pleasure to look at. Rocky would make a low pass over the crop, then pull straight up to do a hammerhead stall, rotate around one wing, and drop straight down to begin his next pass instead of the usual method of turning in a big circle before beginning the next pass. And he could do it all day long.

One day we had a pilot show up in a fairly ragged looking stearman who had heard about Rocky's flying. He considered himself to be the best pilot around and wanted to show everyone he was better than Rocky. So, he came in and asked for a job. Good pilots were always in short supply, and he got hired. He began to work the farms, showing off and trying to duplicate and improve on Rocky's antics.

As time passed, his flying became more erratic, his landings sloppy. He was also a rude person and didn't get along very well with the farmers. Finally, one day he came in hot, bounced two or three times on landing, pulled up to the gas pump, and jumped out with the engine running. He stormed into the office, pulled off his soft helmet and goggles, slammed them down on the counter, and announced he was quitting.

He turned out to be a fairly good pilot, and duplicated a lot of Rocky's techniques, but he just couldn't do it all day long the way Rocky could. He had finally lost his nerve, and that's when he quit. He climbed back in his raggedy aircraft, which was still running, taxied out, took off, and we never saw him again.

Rocky was also popular with the ladies. One day, one of the mechanics and myself were changing spark plugs on the engine of an aircraft parked outside when a car drove up with a couple of ladies in it. Rocky was in the cockpit, getting ready to taxi out, and they ran up to the side of his ship to talk to him. They were good looking ladies, both in short skirts, nice to look at. Finally Rocky gave the engine a couple of blasts to move the ladies away. The whole time the mechanic and I were acting like we were busy on the plugs while watching the whole drama. The ladies just stood there as Rocky swung the tail around at them, then gunned his engine, lifted the tail off the ground, and plastered their dresses against their bodies while he remained motionless on his two main landing gears. They leaned into the prop blast and grinned as he then proceeded to wave the tail at them, while standing still. That is a stunt I have never seen anyone pull off before or since. Finally, with a wave, he released the brakes and taxied out to the runway, holding the tail off the ground during his entire takeoff.

One Sunday I was off and knew that Rocky was working a field close to town. I had my girlfriend, (later to be my wife) with me, and decided to introduce her to my world of aviation. We drove out to the field, climbed on top of a nearby levee to watch the loading operation. I walked up to the ship with Rocky sitting in it, and he yelled at me with the engine still running, "What 'cha doing here, Hoss?" "I came to watch you fly!" I yelled back. He looked over at my girlfriend and grinned, then gunned the throttle and began his takeoff roll.

My girl and I climbed back on top of the levee as he climbed to a little altitude, then did a hammerhead while turning and lined up with the levee. He came straight at us, right on the deck, so low that I grabbed my girl and pushed her down just as he roared over us by just a few feet! She was badly scared, but I just laughed because I knew how good he was, and was proud to know him.

Sadly, years later I heard he got killed down in Mexico where he had gone since he couldn't pass a US flight physical anymore. I was sad to hear about him getting killed, but knew that was the way Rocky would have wanted to go, flying his aircraft on the ragged edge.

My Introduction To Helicopters

Helicopters looked like such weird machines. Noisy, with all those moving parts and things going round and round, with no visible means of support to keep it in the air. I was intrigued by them, but by no means in love with them. As a young Lieutenant with the 101st Airborne Division, with over 500 hours of flying fixed wing aircraft, at tree top level, and a couple of seconds of glider time when I had an engine failure, I was pretty cocky. I wondered why anyone would want to fly such a weird contraption.

One Sunday morning, a fellow pilot asked me if I would like to go along with him on a chopper flight. It seems they had strapped a couple of machine guns on an H-13 helicopter. He was going to take it out to the firing range to see how it performed as a gun platform. He needed some ballast to balance the ship. Always curious, I agreed. I thought it might at least answer some of my questions about these strange machines. Besides, after flying recon aircraft, with no armament, the thought of flying a machine that could shoot back was interesting.

Well, it was more than interesting! I had never experienced such a total sensation of flying like a bird. The freedom the helicopter offered, no requirement for an airport or runway, just simply pull, pitch and go! And the visibility was impressive! There was no engine cowling or feeling of confinement, just a big, clear plastic bubble enclosure. It was almost frightening to look beyond your boots at the ground a couple of hundred feet below.

In an airplane, I always had the sensation of floating, like a sailboat on the top of the ocean. But not in a helicopter. It went along as if it were cutting through the air, going forward and twisting sideways, all at the same time. Not dependent upon the buoyancy of its design, it flew because it willed it with its whirling blades.

Upon arrival at the firing range, he began to fire those machine guns. This experiment later led to the development of armed helicopters which were used in Vietnam. However, at the time, it was all brand new. I had visions of myself as a helicopter ace, shooting down enemy helicopters in a turning, twisting air battle similar to the air combat of WWI, when airplanes were at the same level of development.

I was sold. This was to become my future. I had to get orders to helicopter school. The only problem was I was already on orders to attend Mohawk school. The Mohawk was a twin-engine, twin-tailed, turboprop aircraft, the pride of Army aviation. But I knew the future of Army Aviation was to be found in helicopters, and I wanted to be part of it. I talked my way out of the Mohawk program, and into helicopter school. Thus began my career as a helicopter pilot.

Flying a Bell H-13 with the 101st Airborne

The Ping Pong Challenge

The following story is about persistence over talent. Sometimes you can achieve success by constantly working at it, even if you don't have the latent talent.

This story takes place while I was going through the Army Flight School program. It is a very demanding program, with a 33% washout rate. Each instructor is assigned three students at the beginning of the class, called a stick. By the completion of the pre-flight portion, at least one out of every three has been washed out. Usually, if you received a pink slip on one of your flights, it was the beginning of the end. You had to go up with the class commander and meet his requirements to remain in the program. As a result, all the pilot students were constantly on edge.

I was especially so. The members of your "stick" mates are not only your companions during this trying time, but also your competitors as well. When my two stick mates and I met our instructor for the first time, he asked each of us to introduce ourselves and give a little information about our flying experience to date.

The first to do so was Jack Harter. Jack had a commercial airplane license, a student license in helicopters, and worked as an FAA control tower operator. Jack looked to be a certain graduate.

Next up was Carl Verlander. Carl was ex-Air Force. He had gone through the Air Force flight program up to the point of soloing in jets. Then they found out he was secretly married and had his wife and kids living in a motel close to the base. Since the Air Force required that flying candidates be single until graduation, Carl had violated the rules and was washed out. He completed his Air Force tour and then transferred to the Army to attend the Army flight school program. Verlander wanted to be a pilot in the worst way, and he certainly looked to be a shoo-in.

Then they all looked at me, and I related that I had about 17 hours as a passenger in Civil Air Patrol airplanes, about 3 hours as a student pilot until I ran out of money, and that was it.

All three of them looked at me as if to say, "You're the one, you are going to be the wash-out from this stick." I saw that look, and felt sick to my stomach. To come all this way by getting accepted into flight school, and then to have the most experienced guys in my class as stick-mates was very demoralizing. I went home that night very depressed.

During the lunch break, most of the cadets went to the pilot lounge to eat their lunches, talk about school with other candidates, and generally hang around. There was a ping pong table in the lounge, and the competition was fierce. It was at the table that a pilot could demonstrate his hand-to-eye coordination, and his aggressiveness. The way it worked was that the winner stayed at the table as long as he was winning. The challengers had to wait their turn to get a shot at him. So, you had to play the best guy there, and the learning curve was steep.

Well, I wanted to play. After all, I had played some ping pong at home and in college. I was fairly good, and had won my share of games. So, I got in line to play. The guy playing that day was very good. He had been at the table the whole hour, and no one came close to beating him. When my turn came, he smiled confidently; he was hot, and he knew it. I, on the other hand, felt like a pig going to slaughter. The whole room was watching the known champion against this new boy. I felt like backing out, remembering something or other that I had to do before class. But everyone would know. I had to go through with it.

It was a slaughter. He did not take it easy on me, but beat me to a pulp, laughing at my helplessness at the table. It was very embarrassing. But I played the game to the final shot, which didn't take him long to do. I left the table with my confidence shattered. He didn't just beat me; he humiliated me.

I was under constant pressure at the flight line from my two stick mates who were making flight school look like a piece of cake. They were making the best grades in our class. By comparison, I was barely getting by. Now I had this ping pong defeat to deal with. I could have said, I don't need this, and never played again. But I decided that someday I would beat that guy, and beat him bad. It was part of my determination to get my wings, and to do that, I needed to restore my confidence and will to win.

So, every day at noon time, I would go into the pilots lounge, take my turn at the ping pong table, and take my beating. But I was learning, and every day, the beating became less and less. Soon, the other pilots realized what I was up to, and could see me improving. And so could the champ. The confident smile began to fade. The relief at the completion of each game became more obvious. The room would get quiet when my turn came at the table. No one made any more cute comments about my playing skills (or lack of them). They simply watched me take my lumps as my game continually improved.

My game was improving on the flight line as well. My confidence was coming back. I knew that I would prevail, and I was going to get my wings. I didn't know if it was going to be at the cost of Harter or Verlander, but it wouldn't be me.

Finally, toward the end of our phase of training, I went to the table knowing that today I would win. It was a tight, hard fought, drawn-out game. But I had finally beaten the champ. I was now the champ, the table was mine. I played the rest of that lunch hour, and then never played again. I had accomplished my goals. I graduated from flight school. I got my wings. We were the only stick that graduated intact. Some of the sticks lost all three of their students.

I contribute a lot of my later success in life with the lessons I learned at the ping pong table.

My flight instructor in the back seat in flight school.

The Washed Out Pilot

After months of running through the sand dunes of Ft. Ord, California as an infantry instructor, I finally got the orders I wanted. I was admitted to the Army Flight School Program at Ft. Rucker, Alabama. It meant another trip cross-country with my new wife and baby in a red Alfa Romeo convertible, but heck, I would have walked if I had to. This was the dream I had been working towards during all the years in college and working in the oil refineries.

Arriving in a small Army town that had no reason for existence besides the Army post, we rented a house on a corner lot. It had the necessary screen porch unless you wanted to be fighting mosquitoes day and night. Our next door neighbors were Lt. and Mrs. Frank Harris and family. Frank drove a red Chevy convertible which dwarfed my red Alfa Romeo, but hot pilots had to have red convertibles, no matter the make. Frank was in the same class with me, the Red Hat class. The whole neighborhood was made up of Army officers attending flight school. I joined a carpool with three other Lieutenants who were all in the same class. One of the other Lieutenants was named Feilly. We were moving up in the world. All our friends were college graduates. We had small parties, and these people were all so interesting. We were all driven to graduate, to get those wings! Those wings set us apart from other officers since they also meant flight pay, which meant we were the high-priced guys. What a change for a little Cajun boy who had to work his way through college.

We celebrated my son's first birthday there, and like so many other birthdays to follow for John, and later for Brett, there were kids all over the place, crawling over the floor, faces full of birthday cake and snot, diapers full and smelly, crying as the little boys stole cake from the little girls. But the women at least had company in their misery. They were all the same age, wondering what they were doing in this little southern town, following their soldier boy husbands.

We had fun, but not until the solo period was over. That was a tough time. The pressure to solo was tremendous. You had only so many hours in which to solo, and if you didn't, you were history. This wasn't a civilian flight school course, where you continued as long as it took to solo. Here you had to meet the Army's requirement; if you couldn't do it in the time allocated, they didn't want you.

Meeting the requirements for soloing and graduation was about all the four of us talked about every day as we drove to the flight line together. We knew the wash-out rate was pretty high, 33%, or one out of every four wouldn't graduate. Three of us had little or no experience. The fourth guy had been an enlisted aircraft crew chief before becoming an officer, so he was very familiar with the aircraft, and had many hours in the back seat with a pilot. He was used to flying, knew the aircraft, and was very confident he would be one of those to solo. We all agreed he should have no problem soloing.

We were not so sure about ourselves, but every hour of flying meant we were that much closer to that fated day when the decision was made to let us fly solo. Then, one by one, the rest of us went up for our solo ride while our officer friend was still going around the traffic pattern with his instructor. We no longer talked about who would solo or not while going to work in the morning. The officer just sat there, with a blank look on his face as we approached the flight line.

Finally, one day my instructor, Mr. Williams, told me I had frightened him enough for that day, and climbed out of the aircraft, instructing me to remain. We were sitting on the side of the runway, waiting to taxi out for takeoff when I heard the call of someone on short final for landing. It was our car pool buddy, but his voice sounded different, like he was on the edge of panic. Sure enough, his first pass was too high, and he had to do a go-around. He came back around and tried again, with the same result. This pattern continued until his instructor got on the radio and tried to talk him down. I sat there listening, like everyone else on the airfield, knowing he wouldn't make it.

This was the one guy we were all sure was going to make it, and now came the realization that as much as he knew about flying, he didn't have it in himself to do it. Finally, his voice desperate, but determined, he said he was going to get it down this time. Sure enough, he got the wheels down, then bounced, and bounced again, this time losing all control of the aircraft, finally coming to a stop with the tail up in the air, resting on the nose with a broken propeller. My instructor climbed back in and taxied back to the hanger. That was the end of flying for the day. Our friend did not ride home with us that night.

The next morning, he and his family were gone. The moving van was loading his household goods, but neither he nor his family were around. The remaining three of us all soloed and eventually got our wings. A third of the class washed out, some from flying, some from book grades, and some simply resigned when they realized they didn't have it. My instructor once told me, some people can fly, and some can't, and that's all there is to it.

The Saga Of Don McGowen

As a teenager, I wanted to work during the summer for Louisiana Flyers, a local crop-dusting service working out of the local airport. It was a small general aviation airport which also served Eastern Airlines, the only airline working out of Lake Charles, Louisiana at the time. The airport location across from Chenault Air Force Base made it an exciting place for a young aviation enthusiast to spend his summer months.

During the summer, Louisiana Flyers would hire a young man to work as a hanger helper to fuel, wash, roll-out the ships, sweep the hanger floor, or what-ever was needed to help the operation run smoothly. The pay wasn't great, but for someone who was crazy about airplanes and wanted a career in aviation, it was the only job around.

Unfortunately for me, that job was held by a guy a couple of years older than me, named Don McGowen. He had held the job for a couple of years now, and I couldn't hope to get it until he decided to leave. So, I got friendly with him, and he promised to let me know when he decided not to work there anymore.

One day it happened. Don called me and told me he wasn't going to work there the coming summer, and he had recommended me for the position. Excited, I was at the airport bright and early to apply for the position, and was hired. I held that job for three summers and came into contact with men who were going to become my idols for years to come. Most were ex-WWII pilots like Rocky Taylor, Carl Jack Ernest, and others.

During my senior year in the R.O.T.C. program at McNeese State College, I was appointed the Company Commander of "A" Company with the rank of Captain. I found it interesting to note that my predecessor as company commander was none other than my old Louisiana Flyers friend, Don McGowen. He and I both went on active duty, and I lost touch with him until I arrived at Ft. Rucker, Alabama to begin my flight school training. In the flight school program, each class is issued baseball caps in one of four different colors, red, blue, yellow and green. My class received red hats, since the previous class of red hats was graduating. A member of that red hat class was my old friend, and now a neighbor, Don McGowen. I was beginning to think I was going to follow this guy throughout my flying career.

However, I was assigned to the 101st Division while Don received orders to go to Korea after graduation, and I felt the connection had finally been broken. Word came down that Don had been killed in a plane crash in while on a flight in Korea, but no one knew of any details of the accident. You can imagine how I felt when I received orders to Korea when most of my buddies were going to a small country called Vietnam.

For the first time, I had this feeling of fate and fear; this was getting to be a little much. Was I going to follow in Don McGowen's footsteps all the way to my death? As soon as I got to Korea, I located the unit Don had flown for and went over all the information about his accident. I was determined not to allow myself to get in the same situation. I read the reports, studied the accident photos, even located and flew over the crash site. It wasn't morbid curiosity. I felt I was taking steps to prevent my own death.

He was on a routine mission, which took him over one of the many mountainous areas of Korea. He had an engine failure, and there were very few places for him to land. He must not have been paying attention, because there was a spot or two that he could have made, but instead he elected to try and land on the road below which was cut out of the side of a mountain. It was straight enough for his requirements, and he made a good approach. However, just at touchdown, his right wing-tip hit the side of the mountain, causing his ship to spin around and hit the mountain head-on. Don was killed on impact.

That accident haunted me the entire time I flew in Korea. I did not want to follow in his footsteps to a similar ending. I was prepared, waiting for the engine to quit, waiting to be tested, waiting to break the chain. I was tested and had many close calls, but I survived them all. Maybe it was because I was prepared, expecting the worse to happen, where he wasn't. Or maybe I wasn't supposed to die in Korea because I had further trials to contend with. And there, on a mountain pass in Korea, our paths finally diverged.

Flying With The 101st Airborne Division

Flying with the 101st Airborne was very exciting. This was a unit of risk takers, and they usually looked the other way when their young Lieutenants were doing things that were not approved. Following are a couple of stories of flying in those days. This was before I moved on to flying helicopters and was strictly a fixed wing driver.

The Railroad Track

This incident happened to a friend of mine, Lieutenant Dishman. He was a good pilot, and a nice, quiet kind of guy. He had taken a flight from Ft. Campbell Kentucky to Ft. Bragg North Carolina and back in an L-19 Bird dog. The flight over was normal, but he got delayed there, so was going to have to return at night.

About halfway to Ft. Campbell, over the mountains, the worse scenario happened. At about 5000 feet, at night, his engine quit. Dish, as we all called him, immediately started searching his map and the ground below looking for a landing strip. He couldn't locate any landing strips, but spotted what looked like a road below him. We were used to landing on roads, and to qualify in B phase of flight school, we landed on a lot of roads. So Dish felt he had found a spot to put his aircraft down and started his descent.

The road appeared straight, and he continued down. By this time he was too low to go anywhere else, he was committed. So Dish turned on his landing light in preparation for the landing. What had appeared to be a road when he first sighted it turned out not to be a road at all, but a railroad track! Now it's a known fact that landing gear wheels do not roll smoothly over railroad ties, but Dish had run out of options and continued his approach down to the opening in the woods over the track.

Just before his wheels contacted the railroad, his left wing tip hit a tree, swiveling the aircraft around to the left, and crashing between the trees to come to rest finally with the fuselage intact, minus the wings.

Sadly to say, the accident review board found Dishman guilty of pilot error, and he lost his wings. It was a shame, because he was a good pilot.

The Bridge

Many books and movies show daring pilots flying under bridges; it is a fantasy for many young pilots. But with the 101st, that opportunity presented itself. Our commander was briefing us for a training low level flight across country. We were to fly so low that we had to hop over fences. The idea was that low flying aircraft are harder to hit since the firing opportunity for ground troops is too limited. Every one of us noticed that our flight path took us alongside a river, so we planned on dropping down over the river to get even lower. It so happened that there was a bridge over the river along our route, an opportunity that could not be resisted. Our Commander realized that, and warned every one of us not to fly under the bridge; it was against regulations.

So naturally, I was flying as low as I could and flew my ship over to the river and dropped down to just above the water. And there, ahead of me, was the bridge. The pilings had just enough clearance to fly under it, and wide enough to clear the wings. It was just too tempting, when I might never get another chance like this. I had to do it. I lowered the aircraft even further so my wheels were just inches off the water, aimed for the center of two of the pylons, closed my eyes and flew under the bridge. Talk about a thrill.

When we returned to the airfield, we talked amongst ourselves and realized that about half of the class had taken advantage of that bridge and flown under it. The rest had played it safe and flown over it. It was a risk, but I and others like me had to take it.

The Night Takeoff From A Muddy Road

The unit was out in the field on an exercise aptly called Cold Eagle. It had even snowed that day which turned our road strip into a muddy mess. We were settled in our tents, trying to stay warm when a call came in from the Division staff. Our commanding General had to fly somewhere early the next morning. The L-20 he usually flew in was sitting outside in the woods at this point, and would have to be flown back to the airfield to clean it and get it ready for an early morning flight.

Lieutenant Jim Farrell and I were chosen to fly out of the field that night and return to the airfield. Not only was it dark, but it was also still raining, and we were operating out of a road strip which by now was a muddy mess. The clouds were a low solid overcast, which presented a problem since less than a minute after we became airborne, we were going to be flying in the clouds.

Jim and I agreed that he would make the takeoff which would be tricky in the mud and rain, on a narrow road strip at night. I would be watching the gauges only as he roared down the muddy road, and as soon as he entered the low-lying clouds, I would take over the controls on instruments since the transition from visual to instruments usually takes a while for your eyes to adjust, and we didn't have the time. We found out later that there was a pool going around the unit as to whether or not we would successfully make the take-off. The takeoff required all of Jim's skills to keep the aircraft in a straight line in all the mud until he gained flying speed. At that moment, the aircraft became mine as we entered the clouds and proceeded to climb and return to the airfield on an instrument flight plan, the first one to be filed from a muddy road.

A Hard Landing In A Helicopter At Night

Flying at night was really exciting. Especially on an army post where there are no lights out in the field; it is sort of like flying at night over the ocean. While discussing night flying with an instructor pilot one day, he was asked what we were to do if we had an engine failure in a helicopter at night. "Well, you enter autorotation normally, set up your glide and check your altimeter as you descend. Then when you get about 75 feet above the ground, you flip on your landing light to see where you're going to land. If you don't like what you see, turn it off!" he said with a bland look on his face.

Lieutenant Jim Boyd, a tall lanky red-head with a slow southern drawl, crashed one night while flying a mission over a drop zone. He had picked his ship up into a hover, but got disoriented and for some reason, began going backward. He flew the tail rotor into the ground, and the ship began to spin around a couple of times before finally hitting the ground. The engine and transmission tore loose, crashed forward through the firewall and the bubble canopy, hit his instrument console and glanced off the side of his helmet leaving big gouges in it. The rotor blades were destroying themselves in a frenzy until everything finally stopped. Jim just sat there in the open, the whole plastic bubble was gone, and the aircraft destroyed. Besides the scratches on his helmet, Jim was untouched. Helicopters die hard.

West Virginia Flying

While flying in support of a unit operation in the hills of West Virginia, Nick the Greek had a close one. Flying below the tops of a ridge line on his way back to our isolated airfield located in a narrow valley, he got disoriented (we never got lost) and turned into the wrong valley. It was very wrong, for this valley had high tension wires strung across it at the same height that Nick was flying. When he spotted the wires, he pulled back on the cyclic trying to fly over the wires and miss them. He almost made it.

The tail boom on the helicopter has an airfoil attached to the back of it to assist in lateral direction. It's made of fiberglass and held on by a steel bracket. When Nick flared to go over the wires, the highest wire contacted his ship on this airfoil causing it to pitch forward and his skids actually contacted the wires in a level attitude. The aircraft then bounced up and Nick regained control of the bouncing aircraft and flew it home. The ship was okay, but it took quite a washing to get his pants clean after that incident.

That desolate little airfield almost got me too. I was in an L-20 Beaver, and it was fully loaded. I figured the weight and balance two or three times and realized it was going to be close. It was a short, grass airstrip, at a high elevation, and terminated into the side of a mountain. The technique for this type of take-off was to bring the engine up to full power while sitting on the brakes while the whole aircraft shook and vibrated until you felt you had all the power you were going to get, then released the brakes.

As soon as the aircraft began its roll, I raised the tail wheel off the ground to get more speed. I was constantly judging the speed against the remaining runway as I sped toward the mountain side. Finally, I realized I wasn't going to make it; there was not enough speed and too little runway left. I chopped the throttle and got on the brakes, sliding to a stop just before the end of the airstrip with hardly enough room to turn around because I was so close to the mountain.

I went back to the end of the strip for another try at it. I put the tail of the aircraft off the end, trying to gain a few more yards for my take-off roll. Same program, brakes on, throttle open full, engine roaring, plane vibrating, sweating. Taking a deep breath, I released the brakes and started my take-off roll again. There would be no stopping this time. I was gaining more distance than the last attempt. Feeling the aircraft get light, I hauled back on the yoke as the end of the strip disappeared from my sight under the cowling of the engine. I had rushed it, the aircraft wasn't quite ready to fly, but I was committed. I held the aircraft down, contour flying around the side of the mountain, gaining more airspeed until finally she began to climb out of that narrow valley. Everyone on the ground was watching until we flew out of sight around the side of the mountain, but they were waiting for the sound of a crash. Thankfully, my gamble and technique worked out. I gained airspeed and altitude and cheated that mountain from winning that battle.

However, another L-20 that same day was not successful and did crash into the side of the mountain on takeoff. Thankfully, everyone got out okay, but it taught everyone that that mountain took no prisoners in West Virginia.

Flying With Colonels

The following stories show what happens sometimes when you're flying Colonels. The first story takes place in Korea when I was the DMZ check pilot, and this incident almost got me court-martialed. The second story occurred when I was a member of the 101st Airborne Division and the pilot for a battlegroup commander. Colonels are used to being in charge, no matter where they are, even when they don't have a clue what's going on.

Flying the DMZ tape with a Bird Colonel

Back in 1963, the DMZ in Korea was simply a yellow tape spread out over the countryside marking the boundary between North and South Korea. The tape wandered over hills and down into valleys over countryside that looked the same on both sides. If you were not familiar with it, you could easily fly over the tape accidentally and find yourself in the hands of North Korean soldiers. Prior to my arrival in Korea, an American pilot with a Korean general on board had gotten confused and flew across the tape into North Korea and was captured. Neither has been seen or heard from since.

I had been designated the check pilot authorized to fly the tape on normal patrols, or to take some visiting dignitary who wanted a close hand look at the border. Visitors would arrive at our airfield, and I would brief them before taking off. On most occasions, they would sit back and let me fly them along the tape for miles.

On one occasion a full Colonel arrived at our field and wanted to go to a specific location along the border to meet with some officers of the South Korean army that patrolled there. The Colonel arrived in full colonel mode and after a short briefing mostly conducted by him, we took off and headed north. Arriving at the tape, I turned parallel to it and proceeded to hunt for the meeting place. Finally, the Colonel announced that we were there, and he wanted me to put the ship down at that location immediately. I told him that I could not since that would put us across the border into North Korea. He informed me I didn't know what I was talking about, and to land there immediately. Once again I said, "No Sir," and started looking for another spot to put down. He was not used to anyone telling him no, and started insisting that I land where he wanted, that he was giving me a direct order to do so.

I replied, "Colonel, as long as this aircraft is in the air, I am the aircraft commander and the ranking officer." With that I proceeded to land the aircraft in a spot on the correct side of the tape. As he got out of the aircraft, he turned back to me and said he was going to have me court-martialed when we got back for disobeying a direct order. Then he walked away to join his South Korean officers.

Sometime later, the white faced Colonel appeared with some South Korean officers. He leaned in the ship and apologized for his behavior. The Korean officers had told him that if we had landed where he wanted, we would both be prisoners of the North Koreans by now. The Colonel never mentioned the incident again.

The second Colonel story takes place when I was stationed at Ft. Campbell with the 101st Airborne Division. I was on Stract One, which meant that if anything happened in the world that required the 101st, I would be one of the first to go. While on this assignment, I slept with my duffle bag fully packed next to my bed, ready to go on a minute's notice.

That notice came at o-dark thirty in the dark morning. The voice on the phone simply said, "Let's go" and hung up. I jumped out of bed, slipped on my flight suit and headed to the airfield, not having a clue where we would be going.

At the airfield, I looked up my Colonel and asked him where we would be going. He told me he couldn't tell me; it was top secret. I was stunned by his answer, but replied, "But Colonel, I need to know where we're going to file a flight plan. " No flight plan, he told me. Just get the ship ready for takeoff immediately. I'll tell you when we get in the air.

Being a good lieutenant, I did as I was told and made sure we had a full gas tank and were ready to go, wherever it was. We took off and flew south, and finally the Colonel told me we were going to Oxford Mississippi. I checked my map and couldn't find an airfield by that name. I knew my good friend Ron Wogaman was flying the L20 Beaver with members of the battalion staff on board up ahead of me. So, I radioed him on our private frequency and asked him if he knew where we were going. He replied that they wouldn't tell him either, but to keep flying southward.

I again told the Colonel I could not find any airfield with the name he told me was our destination. He started fussing, complaining that he had a whole battlegroup in the air and didn't know where they were going. He couldn't ask anyone over the radio since the flight was top secret, and since this was before cell phones, he had no way to contact anyone. Finally he said, "Lieutenant, I need to find a landline to call Washington and find out what's going on!"

I always kept track of potential landing spots when I was flying, and knew that there was a small farmer's flying field not too far ahead of us. It was still dark, but had enough ambient light to make it possible for me to land on an unlighted runway.

I informed the Colonel of my plan and began to descend to the grass strip below.

Once on the ground, I taxied toward the hanger, and sure enough, there was an old fashioned phone booth in front of it. I taxied up to the phone booth, stopped and opened the door for the Colonel. I left the engine running as he climbed out and strode up to the phone booth, digging in his pocket since it was a pay phone.

He picked up the receiver and began to talk to someone, then finally he came back to the ship and asked, "Lieutenant, do you have any change?"

The Mountaintop Take-off

This story takes place in Korea at the 3rd Light Aviation Section in a Korean village located 30 miles north of Seoul. It was a unit that flew Korean generals and consisted mostly of Captains, and only two Lieutenants, Jim Spears and myself. A requirement for this posting was a minimum of 500 flight hours and a combat branch. The story points out the importance of briefing passengers on the pilot's intentions prior to take off. Not briefing a passenger can have disastrous results.

It's hot. I'm in the seat of an H-23 helicopter made by Hiller sitting on a helipad on top of a mountain in South Korea. Not only is it hot, but the mountain heliport is also very high, and the density altitude is high. These are factors that can reduce a helicopter to a non-flying machine.

I'm waiting on a communications sergeant, who has been inspecting the radio relay station located on the mountaintop. A call came into our unit on a lazy Sunday afternoon to pick up the sergeant, and since I was the duty officer, I climbed into my helicopter, cranked it up, and took off to begin a long climb to the top of the mountain to pick him up.

As I came in for the landing, I realized that there wasn't much lift at that altitude. I couldn't come to a hover and had to fly the aircraft to touch down on the helipad. Then to top it all off, out walks the sergeant, all 250 pounds of him, and I knew that I would have to use an abnormal takeoff technique due to the lack of lift and the heavy weight.

The sergeant climbed in, buckled up like he had done this many times before, unconcerned, and asked no questions. My plan of action was to use the old hop technique to get off the mountain. This was a piston engine aircraft, no turbine, and the power available was limited. I rolled on full throttle, waited for the engine to develop as much power as it could, then popped the collection up to get the ship off the helipad. With this technique, you utilize a series of hops to walk the ship over to the edge of the helipad, so as soon as the skids were off the ground, you would tilt the cyclic to move the aircraft sideways. This required about four of these hops to reach the edge of the helipad. The sergeant never made a sound during these maneuvers.

The edge of the helipad overlooks a sheer drop off of a few hundred feet of space. Once I had the ship on the edge of the helipad, I took a deep breath, rolled on all the power I could get out of the ship, and popped the helicopter up in the air. Over the side of the mountain, we went into a dive to gain flying airspeed. At this point, we were part of a free-falling, non-flying piece of machinery falling down the face of a mountain.

The sergeant screamed and flung both arms out wide, his left fist hitting me right in the face, so hard my head flew back and hit the firewall. Thankfully I had on my crash helmet with the visor down or he would have broken my nose. But still he almost knocked me out, the ship is in freefall, I'm shaking my head trying to gather my wits. The whole time we're falling I'm thinking, "the accident board will never figure this one out."

Finally my head cleared, my eyes began to function, and I knew I had to take action quickly before we reached the bottom. I took over control, brought back my RPM's, straightened out the ship, and once again became a pilot of a normally functioning helicopter.

Once on the ground at our airfield, the sergeant apologized and said he had never experienced that take-off technique before. I told him it came close to being a one-time experience. (Later in my career, I used this same technique taking off from drilling platforms during hot summers in the Gulf of Mexico.) The sergeant and I were both glad to feel Mother Earth safely under the skids again, even in Korea.

Part III
Petroleum Helicopters

Tail Rotor Failure With Petroleum Helicopters

Down in Morgan City, Louisiana, at the Petroleum Helicopter heliport, I waited outside my Bell 47J model helicopter for my passengers to arrive. The weather was good, and it looked to be a routine flight offshore to deliver my passengers to a rig they were working on.

Finally they showed up with all their gear, and I started to become concerned. These guys were big; I mean really big, mostly muscle. They had to weigh a ton, especially with all their gear. They were hard hat divers, guys that worked underwater in near darkness.

I started re-computing the fuel I could carry, since these guys were so heavy. It meant a smaller fuel load, and I wanted to make sure I would have enough to make it to the first destination, Platform Delta to refuel.

After they all climbed in, I checked the seat belts; it was pretty crowded with those three guys. Then I climbed into the pilot's seat in the front. The pilot's seat was set forward in the center of the aircraft, while the passengers sat on a bench seat behind. I ran through all my checks, and everything looked good, so I called for takeoff clearance and pulled pitch to start our flight.

With the engine straining, I slowly gained altitude, but could only reach 700 feet before I realized she wouldn't climb any higher. It was a combination of heat and a heavy load limiting my performance. But that was OK, 700 feet was enough to get me to our destination, and we proceeded on our way.

As I neared the coastline, something strange began to happen. The ship started to slowly turn to the left. I tried to correct the turn with the rudder pedals, but the aircraft continued the turn, then it increased the rate of turn, and I knew I was experiencing a tail rotor failure of some kind.

The tail rotor is mounted on the end of the tail boom of the helicopter, and it keeps the aircraft from spinning around while in flight. This is a serious failure, and normally results in the aircraft going out of control and spinning down to earth to crash.

I applied right rudder and right cyclic to counter the turn as the helicopter hand book recommends. However, in this cases the book was wrong; it had no effect as the aircraft continued the rotation. Even worse, I was losing rotor RPM. In a helicopter, keeping the rotor RPM within the correct limits is as important as keeping airspeed in an airplane. If the rotor RPM gets too low, the helicopter becomes a falling object, out of control.

The book was wrong. I thought to myself, "Berchman, you had better get creative, or you're going to die!" So I did just the opposite of the recommended procedures. I turned into the spin, applying left rudder and cyclic making the spin even tighter. But my rotor RPM was coming back, and I was regaining control! Now I was really spinning, but I regained control, and judging my height over the ground, I pulled pitch (raising the collective which controls the pitch in the rotor blades) causing the ship to slow its downward descent. By pulling pitch, the aircraft took a tight spin to the left, then slammed into the marsh with a big splash!

I had landed in a marsh, which absorbed a lot of the impact, but the aircraft started to roll to the right when I realized I still had the collective all the way up, and the rotor blades were trying to pull the aircraft up, but only one float came loose from the marsh, causing the ship to roll. I immediately slammed the collective down, and the ship splashed down on both floats. We had made it!

Or so I thought. Just then I received a tremendous blow to my back. My first thought was the engine and transmission had broken loose and had fallen forward through the firewall. Something similar had happened to a friend of mine in the Army after a hard landing.

Then I realized it was the divers; they were pounding me on the back and yelling, "You saved us, you saved us!" Well, I saved them, but they were killing me. They all thought they were dead men when that aircraft came spinning out of the sky.

I unbuckled and climbed out of the aircraft while I still could, and thanked GOD that I had come up with a solution to an unusual aircraft emergency situation by thinking out of the box.

Trying To Find A Place To Land

Anybody see a heliport? Or at least somewhere to land? Locating a place to land can be a problem, but when the place you want to land is constantly moving, offshore about 100 miles, traveling across the Gulf of Mexico from west to east, it can really be difficult.

I was flying out of Morgan City, bringing workmen out to a working barge about 100 miles offshore. I would bring one guy out, and bring another guy in. I was flying a Bell 47-J model which only held a pilot and one passenger. It also had a two-hour range, and the flight one way was a little under one hour. It looked like a pretty simple flight, except for one thing.

The barge was under tow, relocating from one work site to another a hundred miles further east. The dispatcher could not give me the actual location of the barge, much less where it would be when I arrived there in about an hour.

So I plotted the best estimate of its location presently, and then computed using my map and E6-B computer, where it should be one hour from now. My passenger and I strapped in, and off we went. It was a pretty day over the Gulf, lots of sunshine, very little wind to content with, and miles of visibility. A great day to be flying.

An hour into the flight I spotted the barge being towed on the horizon pretty close to where I had figured it would be. After landing, I poured a little more gas in the tank, strapped in my new passenger, and headed back to Morgan City. Once there, I had another passenger waiting for me, but I took time to top off my gas tanks then sit down and try to determine the new location since it would have been traveling for two hours before I arrived on this next trip. A lot of assumptions have to be taken into consideration. Was the speed of the tow constant against the waves and current, and were they holding the same heading? Keeping those things in mind, I pulled pitch and headed for the Gulf and my moving helipad again.

An hour later the barge once again appeared where it was supposed to be. They did not have any more aviation fuel on board anymore, but I had tanked up and had enough fuel to return to Morgan City again for my last passenger exchange.

Everything was still looking good. I landed once again in Morgan City, refueled the aircraft, did my calculations to determine where the barge would be this time, strapped in my last outbound passenger, and headed southeast to find the barge.

I still had about an hour of daylight left, and realized I would have to spend the night on the barge since it would be almost dark when I arrived there. I strained my eyes looking for my wayward barge, checking the time to see if I had arrived at my ETA.(estimated time of arrival). What I had been dreading was now happening. I had flown my estimated course which I felt would place me near the barge, and had covered the distance I felt was required, but there was nothing there. Only the empty Gulf as far as I could see. Using good standard procedures, I continued on course for another 30 minutes without seeing anything.

Now I was starting to get worried. I'm burning up fuel and can't find anything below me but the waters of the Gulf. I begin a search pattern, flying a rectangle that increases in size with each pass while keeping my last known location in sight. The pattern gets bigger and bigger, but the water remains empty.

If I was going to panic, now would be the time to do it. Beginning to run low on fuel, too far over the Gulf to return to Morgan City, and the sun going down in the west, and I've got no place to land.

Of course, I've got pontoons, and could land on the water as long as it stayed smooth. That would require my passenger and myself to spend a wet night seating in a floating helicopter lost in the Gulf. That did not sound appealing to me at all. My only option was to keep searching in the hopes that little floating barge would appear.

Just as I was about to start thinking of putting the ship down in the water, the barge appeared in the distance. That ugly piece of work boat seemed like the most beautiful boat I had ever seen. They had not followed the route I had expected and were quite some distance from where I had anticipated them to be. But at least I had finally located a place to land for the night.

Safe on the helipad on the barge, I tied the aircraft down and went below for a hot meal and strong black coffee. They had an extra bunk, and I went in to sleep while the barge continued traveling. Sometime during the night the barge arrived at its location, and the crew started working. They were pile driving posts down into the bottom of the Gulf to create a platform of some kind. To do that, they had this huge engine to pound the poles down into the ocean floor. So the rest of the night I laid awake while the machine pounded all night long.

The next morning was nice and clear, thank you. The cook served up a hardy breakfast for the hard working crew, and I ate till I was stuffed. The tool pusher got out a map and showed me their location so I could plan my trip back to Morgan City. It was not encouraging; they had moved east quite a ways further than I thought they would, and I realized that I would not have enough fuel to make it all the way back. There was no way to get more fuel to me, since the helipad would accommodate only one helicopter, and just barely at that.

Keeping my fingers crossed, I took off in the hopes of at least reaching the shoreline without running out of fuel. It seemed the ship was flying slower than usual until I could finally see the coast on the horizon. I must have recomputed my fuel load a hundred times as I watched the coast line get closer and closer. Finally, the sand beach passed below the helicopter with nothing below but marsh.

Now the decision was: should I keep flying as long as I could, stretching my gas until the engine quit, and then auto rotate to a landing that was not my choice, or select a good landing spot while still in the air and make the landing with an operating engine.

For once, good judgement prevailed, and I decided to pick a spot in the marsh, land under control, and wait for the company to send another helicopter out with fuel to get me home. Once safely on the ground, I settled in to wait for my fuel to arrive. I had landed in an area which was next to a swamp, and out of the swamp walked a young boy of about 10 or 12. He had seen me land and was fascinated with my flying machine. I was pleased to have someone to talk to and gave him a lesson in helicopter design. I found out he lived in a cabin back in the swamps, had never been to a city or school, and spoke good English, but mostly Cajun. His family hunted and fished, and their only means of transportation was a canoe. But he was very healthy looking and seemed to be happy. An intelligent young man, I wondered as I finally flew out with a tank full of fuel, if he ever left the swamp.

The Rain Storm

The human brain is capable of much more than we presently know. We have tapped only a very small knowledge of its capacity as yet. I found out about some of its vast capabilities while flying at Petroleum Helicopters over the Gulf of Mexico.

While sitting in the ready room in Morgan City, Louisiana, a call came in for a mission to a distant oil field about a hundred miles south of the coast. The weather was not promising, low overcast with isolated rain showers all over the Gulf. I accepted the mission and took a hard look at the overhead while walking out to my aircraft. Once in the air I listened to all the traffic on the radio complaining about the weather.

One of those I heard from was my friend, Frank V. Because of the weather, he had landed on the beach to wait out the severe rain storms which were visible all along the horizon. I spotted Frank sitting down on the sand, rotors turning slowly, waiting for the storms to pass. That was the smart move, but I was reluctant to land, and continued toward the dark sky, my pride telling me a little rain was not going to stop me.

I was always trying to develop new techniques in flying in case I ever got into a situation which wasn't covered in the flight manual. One of my experiments was to keep the helicopter straight and level with my eyes closed, simulating a loss of visibility situation. The problem is a helicopter never wants to go straight and level, and a pilot has to be constantly making corrections to maintain a heading. So, I would place my forearm on my leg, and holding the cyclic very lightly, close my eyes and begin counting. I concentrated on holding the cyclic totally still until I once again opened my eyes after a short count to see if I had wandered off course. Little did I know that technique was going to save me in just a few minutes.

The rain storms were scattered, with lots of room between them, so I continued to work my way to my destination. I was heading for a drilling rig which was located within a field of rigs in a horseshoe configuration, my rig in the center of the semi-circle. It was in sight as I flew inside the opening of the semi-circle when all of a sudden the rain showers engulfed my aircraft, visibility dropped to zero. Here was the real life test of my experiments.

Without thinking, I began to employ my new technique as I slowly lowered the collective hunting for the water below me to give me some sort of visual reference. Finally I could see the water and stopped my descent a few feet above the water, but realized I was heading directly inside the semi-circle of drilling rigs which stood 100 feet above the water. All I could see was the gray of the rain storm, and the water 10 feet below me. I slowed the ship down, and began making a 180 degree pedal turn to get out of that semi-circle of drilling rigs.

Concentrating on making my pedal turn while maintaining clearance over the water, it dawned on me that my mouth was working. I wasn't aware that I was talking, so I had to tune in to myself to hear what I was saying. Imagine my surprise when I realized that I was reciting THE LORD'S PRAYER and wasn't aware of it. One part of me was fighting for survival, while another part was praying for survival, two battles waging inside of me at the same time without my awareness.

Eventually I popped out of the rainstorm and climbed back to altitude. The rainstorm finally ended, and I was in the clear. I had escaped the trap I had flown into thanks to my new technique, and a lot of help from GOD. I learned a lot about the capability of the human mind in the process.

The Frightened Tool Pusher

It was a cold morning in Morgan City, Louisiana. I was sitting in the ready rooms of Petroleum Helicopters. I really didn't want to fly that day, and had nothing scheduled. I was just drinking coffee, reading the paper, totally bored. The chief pilot walked in and told me to report to a ship out on the flight line. It seems there was a tool-pusher who was afraid of flying. (A tool pusher is the boss of the drilling rig; he is like the captain of a ship at sea; his word is law.) He was very particular about who flew him. He had turned down two pilots already this morning. One didn't preflight the ship carefully enough to suit him, and the other didn't do something the way he thought he should when he picked the aircraft up to a hover. The tool pusher tapped him on the shoulder and told him to put it down.

So now the chief pilot wanted me to give him a try. I walked out to the ship, the tool pusher watching my every move as I did my pre-flight. He was trying to decide whether to put his life in my hands. As a pilot, I've always felt free to risk my own life in any way that I wanted, but that I did not have the right to risk that of someone else. I did the best pre-flight I could, his eyes on me the whole time. I carefully and smoothly lifted the helicopter off the ground as if it were an eggshell, ready to break at the slightest mistreatment. I flew steady, smoothly, wanting to make this man feel at ease with my ability and talent. That I wanted to live as badly as he did and wouldn't risk it. Finally he began to settle in, and I could feel his comfort level increase.

But then, halfway there, he tapped me on the shoulder and said, "Aren't you flying a little fast?" I was on the red line of the airspeed indicator, but of course I always flew there. I turned to him and said "I don't tell you how to punch holes in the ground, you don't tell me how to fly my helicopter!" He settled down, and from that day until I left the company, I always flew him. He would not fly with anyone else.

Years later I asked about the tool pusher with the fear of flying, and was told he had gotten killed. A chopper he was in went down, pilot error. I felt sad; the tool pusher must have had a premonition of his fate. But with me, he felt safe. I took that as a compliment to my skill and ability as a pilot, and as a person.

Landing On A Floating Drilling Rig During A Storm

The Seventh Wave

It's raining outside, I mean it's pouring, not a good day for flying. The pilots of Petroleum Helicopters based in Morgan City, Louisiana were just hanging around in the ready room. I was bored to tears. The only flying to be done today will have to be an emergency.

Then a call comes thru; there is an emergency flight coming up, picking up a workman on an LST unit at least 100 miles offshore. An LST is WWII landing craft that is attached to a drilling platform and provides the cooking, sleeping quarters and other facilities for the drilling crew. While the drilling rig is firmly planted on the ocean floor, the LST is floating on top of the waves, held in place by anchors all around the ship.

Not only is it pouring down rain outside, but a strong, almost gale-force wind is blowing out of the gulf. This is not going to be an easy flight. The first stop is Platform Delta, 100 miles offshore, and serves as a refueling and maintenance shop for flights going on an extended flight over water. In those days, we had navigational instruments like they do now, everything was dead reckoning; it was so called because if you reckoned wrong, you were dead.

I volunteered for the flight, since I was bored and looking for something to do. After all, it was just another flight for an experienced pilot like myself, right? So I take off in a 47-Bell helicopter and head for the gulf in the middle of the storm. The first leg is uneventful, and while waiting for the ship to be refueled on Platform Delta, I inquire about the details of my pick-up. I am assured my passenger will be waiting for me on the helipad mounted on the nice, stable drilling platform.

I continue, confident I have made a good decision. Finally the drilling rig comes into sight and I circle the rig determining the best approach to the helipad in all that blowing wind. I take a look at LST, which is pitching and rolling in the storm waves, and say thanks that I don't have to land on that wildly tossing helipad. I continue my approach successfully touching down, and wait for my passenger to climb the stairs to the helipad.

Finally a supervisor approached my aircraft, climbs in to get out of the wind and rain. He informs me that my passenger is actually located on the bouncing LST! So much for my well-planned rescue. This puts landing in a whole new ballgame. The weather is terrible, howling wind, blowing rain, and a landing pad that is bouncing and rolling around like a rubber ball.

I've been had!

The supervisor admits they knew no one would come out if they told the dispatcher the landing had to be made on the LST. I had a few choice words for the supervisor at this point. But I still had the choice of either calling it off, or attempting a landing.

Well, I was assured the passenger had a real emergency, and had to get back to the beach. I decided I had gone this far, so I would at least try to make a pickup.

In the ocean, they have a thing called the seventh wave. You can find a pattern in the wave sequence by counting the waves, and you'll discover that normally on the seventh wave, for a few seconds, the ocean is calm. That would have to be the exact moment I touched down on that LST if I were to make a successful pick-up. I'm sitting on the drilling platform, counting the waves, and sure enough, the seventh wave brings the LST to a complete halt for a matter of seconds. Then it takes a violent dive downward to begin a new series of wild contortions.

I tell the supervisor to tell the passenger to be on the deck of the LST, ready to go, no baggage, so that when I momentarily touch down, to open the door and dive into the aircraft. Don't climb in, dive in, grab on, and hold on since I would be lifting off immediately with or without him.

So I begin my approach, circling the bouncing LST, counting the waves over and over until I felt I had a pretty good feel of the sequence. My passenger was waiting on the deck in the rain, watching and waiting for my approach. Finally, taking a deep breath, I begin my first approach. Quickly I realize my count is off a few seconds, the deck of the LST dives away from under me while just a few feet from touchdown.

I pull up on the collective to climb away from that mad deck and begin my circle again. After a few breaths to steady my nerves, I again resume my count. Feeling more confident with my timing, I once again begin my approach. This time the count is good, the deck becomes motionless, I touch down, the passenger flings open the door and dives in as instructed, grabs the legs of the seat, and hangs on while I immediately begin my climb out. His feet are still hanging out of the aircraft and he pulls himself in, finally sitting down and closing the door as I head back to Platform Delta.

Once settled in, I ask him the nature of this emergency that had brought great risk to both of our lives. He answers, rather sheepishly, "My wife is having a baby."

I've been had again.

The Yellow GTO

The sun is just starting to show its face over the eastern horizon as I drive down the highway to Cameron, Louisiana to begin a shift at Petroleum Helicopters. I'll be based on a pumping platform in South Marsh 28, which is about 80 miles out in the Gulf.

I'm driving my English sports car called a Sunbeam Tiger. It's the only one in Southwest Louisiana, made by an English company called Rootes. There were no dealers in Louisiana. I had bought it through a racing friend who represents the company. It is your typical English sports car, about the size of an MG-A, clean lines, wooden dash, roll-up windows, a modern sports car. The original version is called a Sunbeam Alpine with an underpowered 4 cylinder engine in it. A very tame automobile.

Then Carroll Shelby got into the picture. He's the race driver who had made deals with Ford to make the Lemans winning Ford Cobras and other hybrid race cars. He took that pretty little Alpine, pulled out the small engine, and stuffed a small block Ford V-8 engine in its place, and made it into a Tiger. And it was a Tiger; it could stay with Corvettes and other hot cars of its time. The only exterior signs that it was no longer a docile little English roadster was the word Tiger on the side of the body, twin tail pipes in the rear, and the removal of the small fins to create a sleeker look.

Of course, most people were not aware of the speed potential of this little car; they assumed it was just another little underpowered English car, and that was fine with me. I enjoyed driving this little wolf in sheep's clothing.

The road that leads to Cameron is a two lane blacktop that runs south of Lake Charles, Louisiana through the endless marsh. At one point it crosses the Intracoastal Canal that runs across south Louisiana. At that time there was no bridge, just a small ferry that handled 2-3 cars per trip. As I pulled up, there were a couple of cars in line, waiting for the next trip. One was a school bus, and the other was a yellow

GTO. Finally, the ferry arrived on our side, unloaded, and the three of us drove onto it and sat waiting to cross.

After we arrived on the other side, the GTO blasted around the school bus and drove out of sight. I waited until there was no oncoming traffic and pulled out to go around the school bus also. Then as I prepared to pull into the front of the school bus, there sat the GTO. He wouldn't let me in. So I speeded up to pull in front of him. He speeded up also, and kept me in the left lane. I looked over to see a young man grinning at me, and I knew he wanted to race; the young woman sitting next to him was egging him on.

I speeded up a little more, and so did he. We kept going faster and faster until we were both in excess of 100 mph. He started looking at me with a different face. Little Sports cars were not supposed to go this fast! He began to get a worried look, and the girl was not happy anymore. We were now approaching a sweeping right hand curve and going 120 mph last time I looked at the speed odometer. I wasn't worried, I had raced sports cars around fast tracks and knew how to go around high speed corners. But the driver of the yellow GTO was a street racer, strictly a straight line racer, no corners, and certainly no curves at 120 mph. As we got closer, he began to look back and forth to me, hoping that I would back off, but I kept my foot on the floor. By this time his lady friend was screaming at him, and I waited for him to give in. Finally, he let up and with a roar, I zoomed in front of him and went around the curve while maintaining my speed. I could hear his engine backing off as I left him far behind.

I arrived at my heliport which was located alongside the highway and pulled in next to my ship. The young mechanic was outside as I pulled up and was admiring my red Tiger. The sound of a strong engine at idle made both of us look toward the highway to see a yellow GTO slowly driving by.

"Look at that, that's the fastest guy around here," he said.

"Not anymore" was my only response.

80

Part IV
Los Angeles Airways

Moving Up Into Heavier Equipment

Friday afternoon, the end of a ten-hour shift with Petroleum Helicopters. I flew my ship to the heliport in Cameron, Louisiana for a checkup and refuel before flying back to the offshore platform I was assigned. While I was waiting for the mechanics to check out my aircraft, another helicopter came flying in for a fuel stop. It was my flying buddy, Frank Vranicar.

He proceeded to tell me that this was his last shift with PHI; he was going to California to fly passenger-carrying helicopters for an airline called Los Angeles Airways. I had never heard of it, but the more he told me, the more I liked it. They were flying S-61s, a twin-engine turbine helicopter carrying 32 passengers and a crew of 3. It flew all over the Los Angeles basin delivering passengers to helipads from Disneyland to Riverside. It was a regular airline job with all the perks.

I was ready to leave PHI. I found out that there was no way to advance as a result of your flying skills or performance. I had managed to safely land a ship with a tail rotor loss with no damage to passengers or the ship. My bonus for getting a damaged aircraft down in one piece was a cigarette lighter, and I don't smoke.

Meanwhile, another pilot had made a pilot error and dumped an aircraft in the Gulf after misjudging a takeoff from a drilling platform, which totally wiped out the aircraft. I found out later that he and I were making the same amount of money.

I asked my supervisor why the same amount of money for such a wide disparity of performance. His reply was that it had nothing to do with job performance, but only with our respective hire-on date. At that point, I knew I had no future with PHI.

After Frank departed on his way to Galveston, I flew back to the platform and thought more about the airline job. I had to give it a try. A job like that would also be better for my family, flying for a living, but home every night, as opposed to ten days on and five days off like I was presently doing with PHI.

I picked up the phone and called long distance to speak to the operations manager of Los Angeles Airways, Boyd Kesselring. He asked me about my flying history and why I wanted to work for them; finally, he asked me if I could be there Monday morning for an interview. I said I could, but I want to tell you one thing. "What's that?" he asked. "I'm not tall enough to pass most airline height requirements." His reply was, "I don't care how tall you are, I just want to know if you can fly helicopters." I replied, "You're talking to the world's best helicopter pilot!"

I flew out to California and got the job as a co-pilot. I got busy making arrangements to move my family out, get an apartment, along with all the domestic stuff required for such a move. Not long after I got the family all settled down, my Grandfather, Willis Lormand, or Pa as we all called him, passed away. My father called, and being a man of few words, simply said, "Come home."

I went to see Mr. Kesselring to request permission to go home for the funeral. He told me a grandfather does not qualify as next of kin, and he could not authorize me leaving to attend the funeral. In fact, he couldn't guarantee I would have a job waiting for me when I returned. I told him I was sorry, but where I come from, a grandfather who has been head of the family, does qualify as next of kin, and I was going to return for the funeral.

I went back to Louisiana for the funeral after relocating my family to California and now not even sure I had a job to return to. But, as the oldest grandson, I was expected to be there, and I fulfilled that obligation. It was with a sad face that I opened a letter from Los Angeles Airways a day after the funeral, expecting the worse news since they told me there was no guarantee that I still had a job waiting for me. Imagine my joy when inside the envelope was a return trip ticket paid for by Los Angeles Airways. I knew then I had made the right decision by going to work for such an honorable company.

A 32-passenger S-61 at Los Angeles International Airport

The Reserve Co-Pilot

It was still dark outside on that early California morning when I heard the car horn telling me it was time to go.

My friend, Jack Dupuis, was waiting outside to take us to Los Angeles International Airport where we would board our S-61 passenger carrying helicopter and spend the day flying together. Jack was a Captain for Los Angeles Airways, a helicopter airline that flew all over the Los Angeles basin delivering passengers to various heliports. Today I was to be his co-pilot.

I always looked forward to flying with Jack. He was a Louisiana boy, easy to be with, but demanding to fly with. Jack did everything by the book, the check list was to be followed before each flight, the co-pilot reading the items while Jack repeated each item as he selected and flipped the various switches.

He believed in creating as smooth a flight as possible for the passengers, no show-off stuff, just good, smooth, professional flying. He was a senior Captain with thousands of flight hours, and I was a senior co-pilot at the time.

When we got to the airport, our dispatcher told me I would be pulled off the line to fly with our chief pilot, Mr. Ron Crawford. I was in training to become a Captain and was to take a check ride with Ron. A reserve co-pilot Terry Herrington, would be called in to take my place with Jack. Although I was disappointed, I was looking forward to becoming a Captain myself and was ready and looking forward to the check ride.

During the check ride with Mr. Crawford, we received a call from our dispatcher. He sounded nervous, and reported that he had received reports of a helicopter crash in the area and requested us to fly to the site to verify if there was a crash or not.

I was at the controls as we spotted the crash site, circling counterclockwise so Crawford could get a good look out of his side of the aircraft. My heart sank as he confirmed it was one of ours. Then the dispatcher came on the radio and verified that it was Jack Dupuis that had gone down.

His ship had lost a rotor blade, and the aircraft at that point was uncontrollable. Everyone on board had been killed. I was circling, looking down on the crash site, realizing that by a quirk of fate, that could have been me down there.

When Crawford and I landed, I was asked to take Jack's mustang and go pick up his daughter and drive her back to her mother's home in Orange County. I didn't even have time to call my wife and let her know I wasn't in that aircraft. She knew the flight number of my schedule and they were reporting it all over the news, so I wanted her to know I had been rescheduled. The dispatcher said he would call her for me and let her know I was alright.

When I finally returned home later that evening, I found my wife almost in hysterics. She had heard about the crash on the radio, and not long afterwards, my father had called from Louisiana asking if I was involved in that accident. She told him the company office had told her I was okay, and my father asked, "Did you talk to him yourself?" That created doubt in her mind and once again, she became upset until I drove up to the front of the house. This was the second time I had been involved in an aircraft accident that made national headlines, and both times my father in Louisiana heard about it on the radio before I had a chance to call home.

Once again I was reminded how fragile life is, and how we need to enjoy every minute we have, since we don't know how many minutes we have been given. I have thought many times of the reserve co-pilot, who had been happy to take my place in the helicopter with Jack, not knowing what fate awaited him on that beautiful California morning.

The UFO Experience At Los Angeles International

A lot of pilots you talk to have some kind of story about UFO's. Some claim to have actually seen one while flying. I must confess I haven't seen one, but I have experienced one. It happened while I was flying with Los Angeles Airways in the late 60's.

I had the late night run, which meant the last flight of the day would be coming into Los Angeles International well after dark. On this occasion it also meant dense fog, the kind of fog that is found on the coastline of California.

As a result, we were making our approach to LA International under instrument conditions. Visibility was zero, which meant we couldn't see a thing outside of the windscreen. I was flying the ship, and talking to approach control. We were not on a glide path on anything, but just following the instructions of the controller as he led us toward the airport off to the side of the glide path and out of the way of faster overtaking airliners.

When working with controllers in situations like this, everyone is very quiet. Instructions for turns to new headings are given in a soft, quiet, professional voice. An example would be like, "LA 277, turn right to a new heading of 285." You would reply "Roger, 277 right to 285, over."

The air was smooth, and everything was proceeding normally; it had been a long day, and we were looking forward to shutting down, unloading, and heading home. Suddenly, the controller came on in a whole different tone of voice, almost yelling "LA 277 turn right immediately!" No heading change or anything, just turn right immediately. I immediately moved the cyclic over to the right, putting the aircraft into a hard right turn; in the next instant, the big aircraft was pitched around like a small boat in an angry sea! Our instruments were going wild as I fought to control the bouncing aircraft and continue the turn. After the bouncing settled down, the controller came back on the air and said to stop our turn. I rolled the aircraft straight and level, and waited. Finally, he came back on and asked what our heading was. I told him, and he had me turn back left onto a new heading to complete our approach.

I got on the radio, and asked without announcing my call sign, "What was that?" "A UFO" was his reply.

After safely landing, the ground controller came on and told us to report to the FAA office immediately upon landing. We got in a car and drove over to the FAA office where we were told not to write up that near miss. We reminded them that anytime there was an incident like that, we were required to make a report. Once again, we were told in no uncertain terms, to make no written report, and forget about it. But they did tell us that a large, unknown object had flown through our airspace, and only our quick reaction had avoided a collision. It was unannounced, flying at a high rate of speed, and in their opinion, it was a UFO.

So, although we didn't see anything, I felt I had gotten up close and personal with a real Unidentified Flying Object that cold, foggy night over Los Angeles.

Part V
Lockheed California Company

A Working Pilot

It takes many years for a pilot to build up a lot of flight time. Along the way, it means the pilot will risk having an accident. As flight time increases, so does confidence of having avoided dumb mistakes which can end a pilot's career.

A working pilot comes up through the ranks. First, flight school, then experience to gain enough hours to get that first flying job, (one where someone actually pays you to fly!) then you move up to fly bigger and more sophisticated aircraft as you gain hours and experience.

My first experience with aircraft was as a 5 or 6 year old when my father brought me to a field out in the country where they were conducting war maneuvers prior to WWII. The Army had taken over central Louisiana with soldiers, tanks, and cannons everywhere. We came across a fog shrouded field that was being used as an airfield for light observation aircraft. These small canvas-covered aircraft were taxiing over the rough ground, their engines growling with impatience, as I stood there, captured by these small, frail aircraft getting ready to take to the air.

I never forgot the image of those aircraft in the fog for the rest of my life. And my father introduced me to the love of my life.

Years went by, Boy Scouts with all my buddies, camping in the woods, and earning badges until I achieved the Life status. Then it was time to move up to the Explorer Scouts. But I had had enough of camping in the woods, and sleeping in tents. I wanted to take to the air. That was when I learned about the Civil Air Patrol.

Eventually, I was promoted to Cadet Captain and took part in search and rescue missions, even getting rides in the back seats of observation aircraft. We even developed a drill team which took part in numerous parades within the local area. One of our members, Johnny Odom, became an airline pilot years later.

Membership in the Civil Air Patrol led me into contact with real airplanes, flown by real pilots. That led to a summertime job working as a hanger helper at the local crop dusting outfit called Louisiana Flyers. They flew beautiful Stearmans, painted green and white, and I got to climb all over them. Flown by real pilots, most of whom were ex-WWII fighter pilots, and they could do anything in those beautiful bi-wing aircraft. Watching them was a treat for a young man like me.

Then came college, Army ROTC, and a chance to enter the Army flight school program. That was not as easy as I expected, since my two table mates were already graduates of civilian flight training. Cadets Verlander and Harter were getting great grades while I was struggling, even got a pink slip and came close to washing out. The wash out rate at that time was 33%. But I overcame that bad grade, and went on to get my wings. We were the only table where all three successfully completed the course. Most tables had at least one or two of the cadets not make it. I graduated as a fixed wing pilot, and had finally gotten wings of my own.

While serving with the 101st Airborne, I got an opportunity to receive additional training as a rotary wing pilot, and that began my love affair with helicopters. As an experienced dual-rated aviator, I got an assignment to Korea, and became a member of the 3rd LAS (Light Aviation Section) which was stationed at I Corps Headquarters 30 miles north of Seoul. We flew a lot of high ranking officers, including Korean generals. Captain Nutter was the private pilot of General Chun, the commander of the Korean forces in that area. I became the DMZ check pilot. The DMZ at that time was not a fence, but yellow tape laid on the ground between the two countries. So, if an officer wanted to visit Korean troops stationed on the DMZ, they would fly into our airfield, get into a ship with me, and I would fly the tape. That gave me the opportunity to meet with many Korean soldiers, and even play ping pong with them. They always won; their table was longer, and they were very accomplished at slams. But flying the tape was tricky, and if you flew over it, the North Koreans would seize you and you were never heard from again. This has actually happened to a couple of Army pilots.

My tour of duty in Korea led to a large increase in flight hours. I became the company maintenance officer and test pilot. When a ship came out of overhaul, I had to take it up and make sure everything was working right. Many days I spent all day jumping out of one aircraft and into another, from airplane to helicopter. It was a great assignment.

After my career in the Army came to an end, I returned to Louisiana and got a job flying offshore with Petroleum Helicopters. This was an interesting job, flying over hundreds of miles of open water with no navigational aids, just a floating compass and dead reckoning, finding helipads located on drilling rigs hundreds of miles offshore. I added to my experience level not only in hours but in confidence as I experienced many exciting adventures including loss of a tail rotor while flying three very big, hard helmet deep sea divers. We came spiraling out of the sky, and with a lot of luck (99%) and ability, (1%) I managed to get the ship down safely on the edge of the marsh in one piece. My bonus for successfully saving the aircraft and passengers was a cigarette lighter! And I don't smoke.

With the experience and hours that I had now accumulated, I applied and received a job flying large, twin engine, airline passenger carrying helicopters operated by Los Angeles Airways. We carried at least 32 passengers and 3 crew members all over the Los Angeles basin, from Los Angeles International to Riverside, California and other helipads in between. It was a regular airline job, gaining instrument ratings in helicopters as well as an Airline Transport Rating. I had a couple of new experiences, loss of an engine, and got caught in Instrument conditions while flying Visual Flight rules, but overall it was pretty boring flying. It was the same routes every day, and same time schedules, but I still enjoyed the gift of flight, in a big beautiful aircraft.

One of the aircraft I was scheduled to fly one day had a main rotor failure, and everyone on board got killed. I had been taken off the flight to receive Captain training that day, which saved my life. The Captain (Jack Dupuis) from Louisiana had driven me in that day since we had been scheduled to fly together. You can imagine how I felt that evening when I had to drive his car back home to his wife.

Then I experienced the future. A group of our Captains were invited to review the state-of-the-art helicopter that a Lockheed California company was building. It captured my imagination! It had wings, a pusher prop, a rigid rotor system, and it was designed from the ground up as a combat aircraft. And it flew at the unheard of speed at that time of 250 knots, straight and level. I had to fly it!!

One night afterwards, while flying with a Captain, we had a conversation about that advanced helicopter, and what it could bring to the world of helicopters. I told him I really wanted an opportunity to fly that aircraft. He responded, "Then why don't you apply for a job there?"

I replied, "I never thought of that. I'm not a test pilot. I'm a working pilot. They would never hire me."

"Why not?" he said. "You're very experienced, and weren't you a test pilot for your unit in Korea? And besides, all they can say is NO." That did it; I decided to apply.

Now, aircraft companies normally hire pilots who are graduates of a military flight test program. But I applied anyhow, even though I was just a simple, up through the ranks working pilot. I had a highly qualified license, with an airline transport rating with an instrument ticket in both helicopters and airplanes. But compared to the other applicants, I was a novice.

I went through a series of preliminary interviews, and was then scheduled to be interviewed by the chief test pilot of the Lockheed

Aircraft Company, Tony LeVier. Mr. LeVier wrote the book, *Test Pilot*, based on his many experiences in experimental aircraft. He had made the initial flight on many state-of-the-art aircraft and was lead pilot for many aircraft like the twin-tailed devil of WWII, the P-38, and the first operational jet fighter, the Lockheed P-80 shooting star which saw action in the Korean conflict. He had worked directly with Kelly Johnson of the skunk works organization, the top secret part of Lockheed responsible for the state-of-the-art aircraft in service at that time.

He was very polite and asked how to pronounce my name, Berchman Richard. When I told him, he had a funny look on his face which I couldn't understand. Later, after reading more about him, I discovered his mentor was named Milo Burcham, which sounded a lot like Berchman. Milo got killed testing the P-38. The top scoring ace in the Pacific war during WWII, flying a P-38, was Richard Bong. Mr. Bong came to work at Lockheed after the war, and got killed in a P-80 when he had a flame out on takeoff. To this day I believe that the recognition of my name to Mr. LeVier had a lot to do with his hiring me. After all, I was a small man, nothing glamorous about me, just a working pilot who came up through the ranks loving to fly, just like they did.

Three Cheyennes in formation. I'm sitting in the back pilot's seat of the lead aircraft. The middle aircraft is flown by Ray Goudy, an ex-U-2 test pilot, and the third aircraft is piloted by David Beal. That is the aircraft in which he was killed later in the program when it came apart on an envelope expansion test. That was the only time that three aircraft had a chance to fly in formation over Oxnard, CA.

The Rescue Mission In The L-286

After leaving Petroleum Helicopters in Louisiana, I was now flying for a real helicopter airline in California, Los Angeles Airways. Recently promoted to Captain, I had four stripes on my sleeves, and braid on my cap. I was a proud little Cajun. We were flying 32 passenger, twin-engine turbine helicopters made by Sikorski designed as S-61. We flew into heliports located all over the Southern California basin, from Burbank to Riverside, and south to Newport Beach. It was a great job, flying almost every day but home every night.

Then the company received an invitation to have their Captains tour the Lockheed plant in Van Nuys to view their latest project, the rigid rotor AH-56A Cheyenne helicopter gunship.

Up until that time, I had never thought much about who built the birds we flew. I knew that some had different characteristics, but always figured that was the result of the design, not the maker. It was really interesting to see what it took to get a design off the drawing board and into the air.

I was most impressed by the rigid rotor concept, and the plans Lockheed had for it. For me, and for a lot of others in the industry at that time, it could change the face of short-haul aviation as we knew it then. They were building a gunship, the first gunship incorporating armor, night-vision systems, laser guided weapons, tow-missiles, and helmet sights for the belly-turret gun. It was 73 feet long, had wings, and a large pusher prop to push it to speeds over 240 knots. This was something, since few helicopters at that time could exceed 140 knots.

Their next step was to create a passenger-carrying version of the gunship, which would be as large as the ships we were presently flying, the Sikorsky S-61. Both aircraft were 73 feet long, so it was simply a case of a different fuselage and an additional engine, but an increase of speed of more than 100 knots and the smoothness of the rigid rotor system.

Now, I figured, since I was the world's best helicopter pilot, it only stood to reason that I should be flying the world's best helicopter. One night on a regular trip to Disneyland, I told my Captain, Bob Prime, that I wanted to fly the Lockheed ship. But to do so, I would have to quit my job at LA AIRWAYS. I had just been promoted to Captain, and my life and career seemed fixed. Besides, I was not a graduate of a test pilot school, I was just a working pilot who came up the ladder the hard way. But Bob encouraged me. He said if I was serious, I should apply; after all, they could only say no.

I applied, and no one said no. Finally, I was interviewed by one of the greats, Tony LeVier. He was the chief test pilot at Lockheed, and had played major roles in the development of the famous P-38, the P-80 shooting star, and many other Lockheed aircraft. He seemed to be taken back by my name, Berchman Richard, which I didn't understand at the time. But I got the job, and was elated.

Later I read his book, *Test Pilot*, and found out that two of his best flying friends were Milo Burcham, and Richard Bong. Both had been killed while flying as Lockheed Test Pilots. My name must have struck a chord in his memory.

So began my Lockheed flying career. I had doubled my salary and been elevated to a place in my career that I had never dreamed possible. Of course, I did not immediately go into flight testing. I was delegated to fly the L-286, which I'll cover in another chapter. It was a one-off ship that Lockheed built to demonstrate the rigid-rotor concept. We would take up visiting big-shots and wring it out, showing the capabilities of this new rotor system. When someone asked me how it worked, I would just look up with reverence at the rotor and say, "It's magic." That usually resulted in a stunned look on the face of the person, many of whom were of the engineer profession, or military and were not used to those kinds of comments about technical items. But it did get their attention and made them remember me.

I had a lot of adventures in the L-286, but the one that really brought me to the attention of upper management happened during the rainy season in Los Angeles. It had been raining for days, the clouds were low, overcast, and gray. Rain was coming down in sheets, and there was nothing for pilots to do but spend boring hours in the pilots' shack doing paperwork.

Then a call came in. Someone was having a heart attack up in the Sand Canyon area and needed a helicopter to get him to a hospital. This was a very unusual request since the L-286 was a very special bird, and not normally used for flights not connected with Lockheed business. But it seems that all the helicopters in the LA Basin were in use for various rescue missions. I was third in line when the call came in to take the flight. Both Dave and Doug Devine, my bosses, turned down the flight for different reasons. I knew why, they didn't want to risk damaging the 286 in that terrible weather, for it would mean the end of your career at Lockheed to hurt that ship. But I was bored, and after a couple of years of flying in rainy weather in the Gulf of Mexico, the rain didn't bother me. So I accepted. I got a good flight test engineer, Bill Groth, to go with me to help navigate, and we took off in a driving rainstorm for a rescue mission.

I headed for the pass towards Valencia, but the clouds were below the tops of the pass, and the pass was littered with high-tension wires. That route was closed. We had turned around and were heading back to cancel, but I changed my mind. I wanted to complete the mission, especially since it meant saving someone's life. I thought of the pass into the Simi Valley. I knew it well since I had driven through it only a few weeks earlier. We headed to it only to find it was also socked in. But the pass is a cut through the hills where the highway goes through, and there was an opening just high enough to let the cars through. So I dropped down to a few feet above the roadway, and very slowly, we made it through the pass without encountering any autos.

Another pass awaited us, and this one required me to contour fly by following down the side of the winding road to the valley floor below. But once on the valley floor, we were on our way. We located the house which was at the end of a cul-de-sac. The police were keeping the end of the street open for us as I made my approach. It was a tight landing on a city street, with only one way in and out. The patient was loaded in while Bill computed our remaining fuel. He discovered we did not have enough fuel to go back the way we had come. We needed another way home, and the pass was still closed.

The mountain range dividing the Sand Canyon area from the San Fernando Valley is quite steep, and the winds were blowing hard. I remembered that there was a fire station on the ridge line above us, and called them to see what their weather was like. As I had guessed, the wind whipping across the top of the ridge had created an opening of about 10 feet over their heliport. Using a technique I learned while flying in a snowstorm in Korea, I flew the chopper up the side of the mountain, using the tops of the trees as my reference point until we reached the heliport. We zipped over it at about 10 feet, rotor blades in the bottom of the clouds, and began a descent down the other side to Burbank. This led us over the reservoir and into the Valley.

102

Now the problem was, did we have enough fuel to make it to the Burbank airport? The fuel warning light was now glowing brightly, and we both were beginning to feel the pucker factor increasing. I called Burbank tower and requested an emergency straight-in approach, and an ambulance to be waiting for our patient. I made a sliding landing, afraid the engine would quit at any minute. Just as the ship came to a complete stop safely on the tarmac, the engine quit. Later, when we tried to restart the engine to move the aircraft, it wouldn't start. There was nothing but fumes in the fuel tank. Tony, the assigned mechanic for the L-286, later said he had never put that much fuel in the aircraft.

It turned out later that our patient was the personal doctor of many of the top level executives at Lockheed, and Bill and I received a lot of attention for our daring but successful rescue.

The Lockheed 285 Rigid Rotor Helicopter

The Lockheed California Company built a couple of beautiful helicopters to test the rigid rotor concept. They were named the L-286. One was used to set helicopter world speed records with Chief Test Pilot, Don Segner. The engineers mounted a jet engine on one side of the helicopter in addition to the smaller internal jet engine. Since the ship had a rigid rotor system which gave it tremendous stability, the heavy offset engine did not harm the handling characteristics of the ship. It proved to be successful, and Don became the fastest helicopter pilot in the world as a result.

The other ship was built for demonstration purposes. It became the first helicopter in the world to do loops and rolls as it was demonstrated at the Paris Air Show in 1966. Old time Lockheed test pilot, Sammy Mason, became the first helicopter pilot to successfully demonstrate a pure loop and live to tell about it.

The L-286 was a 4-place ship with retractable skids; it was very slick looking for its time, fast, stable, and comfortable.

One morning I was assigned a flight in the L-286 from Van Nuys to Los Angeles International to carry a very important VIP. It was a typical San Fernando Valley day, with a little ground fog mixed with yellow smog. I had to declare a special VFR clearance to climb on top of the haze layer before proceeding to LA International. The passenger arrived just barely in time to complete the flight. I pulled pitch as soon as he was strapped in his seat.

We climbed up through the smog with no problem, but just as I cleared the haze layer, the aircraft had a violent kick 90 degrees sideways, then just as violent, back to center. It felt like some sort of transmission failure, so I immediately declared an emergency situation and began an autorotation back down to the heliport. While coming down, I switched channels and notified ground control to get a vehicle for the VIP otherwise he would miss his flight, then back again to the control tower.

The autorotation was safely made, the passenger departed, and made his flight just barely. Then the investigation began to determine what had happened. I explained what had happened, but the mechanics and engineers could not find anything wrong, and I couldn't duplicate the maneuver in the air. I wrote up the incident which required a full tear-down to find the problem. Again, nothing wrong was found, and the aircraft was placed back on flyable status. However, from that point on, I was not the preferred pilot for the L-286 since I was the new boy and had probably made a mistake. Mistakes by pilots are frowned on at Lockheed.

One day my boss had to fly the L-286 down to the Yuma Proving Grounds test facility in Arizona with a passenger. Half way there, he experienced the same hard over that I had experienced. He put the aircraft down in the desert, which resulted in a major project to get the aircraft back to Van Nuys.

This time, on the subsequent tear-down, they found the problem. One of the hydraulic servos controlling the tail rotor had experienced a hard-over, going from one extreme position to the other in a split second.

I was now cleared of any mistake, and had demonstrated my integrity for refusing to change my report of the problem. I feel this is one of the reasons that Lockheed later approached me about becoming an engineering test pilot on the AH-56A Cheyenne helicopter test program.

Don't Play Around With A Full Throttle

Sometimes we get a little too cocky. In a race car, you begin to drive fast before the tires are warmed up, and you don't realize it until you enter a fast turn and the car doesn't respond to your turning the steering wheel; it just continues in a straight line, right into the wall. Equipment sometimes takes longer to warm up than humans do. We get excited and want to get going, but the equipment has its own schedule, and cannot be rushed. This is what happened to me one sunny afternoon at the Lockheed Flight Test facility in Oxnard, California.

I was sitting in the cockpit of the AH-56A Cheyenne gunship with my flight test engineer, Donald Upton, in the front seat. I had just taxied out onto the runway in preparation for the takeoff. It was the third flight of the day, and the two previous flights had been without any problems at all, so I was very confident in the ship. I decided to see just how fast this ship would accelerate. I knew it would be fast, but normally I increased the speed gradually to be prepared if anything was to go wrong. In flight tests, you don't push your luck any more than you have to.

So, I brought the ship into a hover three feet off the runway, reached down to grasp the beta throttle control, and twisted it quickly to the full throttle position. Immediately, the ship leaped forward like a dragster, slamming me back into my seat much harder than I expected. But then the unexpected happened, my seat brackets broke from the violent acceleration, and the seat slid back to the most rearward position.

I am a small man, and usually fly with my seat adjusted to the most forward position. Now, I'm in an aircraft that is screaming down the runway, three feet off the ground, and I can't reach the controls. Donald and the pilots in the chase plane flying above us are yelling, "What is going on Berchman?" They knew that at that rate of speed, if I didn't begin a climb out soon, I would run off the end of the runway.

Let me take a moment here to explain something about the Cheyenne helicopter. It is a very stable aircraft, thanks to the capabilities of the rigid rotor system. I found that it would maintain any attitude you placed it in indefinitely. Unlike any other helicopter flying at that time, no auto pilot was required. So thankfully, the ship held its heading and altitude as it zoomed down the runway at 3 feet.

Located at the top of the cyclic control is a trim tab. The cyclic is the control stick that is used to fly the aircraft, turn right or left, nose up or nose down. It is very sensitive, and allows you to make very small corrections in the aircraft's attitude. I couldn't reach far enough to grasp the cyclic since I was tightly strapped in the seat, but had to do something to initiate a climb before I ran out of runway. I twisted sideways in my seat, reached out with my forefinger, and touched the cyclic trim tab. Very carefully, I beeped the trim tab rearward to raise the nose and begin a climb. It had to be gently; too much and the aircraft would have gone too nose high into a stall or even flipped all the way over.

Finally, the nose began to rise, and the ship began to climb for altitude. Donald and the chase plane pilot were still calling on the radio, asking what the problem was, but I couldn't reach the mike button. After I had the ship trimmed into a climb attitude, I unbuckled my harness and parachute, found a part of the cockpit that I could grab, and pulled myself, seat and all, back up to a forward position. I re-strapped myself in, then once again took hold of the controls and leveled the ship out.

That terminated the test, and we returned to land. The engineers had to figure out why my seat broke loose the way it did. It could have resulted in a very bad crash, since we could have impacted the ground at a speed in excess of 200 mph the way we were accelerating. The stability of the Cheyenne, and that little trim tab, saved my life for another day.

Sammy Mason – A Christian Test Pilot

At the Paris Air Show in 1966, history was made by a Lockheed Aircraft Corporation test pilot when he performed the first complete loop in a helicopter and lived to tell about it.

This wasn't an ordinary test pilot, or an ordinary helicopter. The test pilot was Sammy Mason, an old time test pilot who had flown in the days of bi-wing airplanes, in air shows, barnstorming, and in many aviation movies of the day.

His aircraft that day was a new and different type of helicopter. It was called the L-286 and utilized a new type of rotor system, the rigid rotor. It minimized the working parts of the rotor system which was developed by Lockheed. This new rotor system allowed the aircraft to fly upside down, do loops and rolls, and any other aircraft maneuvers that regular helicopters could not do.

As a young curious test pilot, I was fortunate to be able to spend some time with Sammy as we played chess in an abandoned control tower on the grounds of the Lockheed California Corporation airfield in Van Nuys, California during our lunch hour. We had many interesting talks about his flying experiences in the early days of aviation. It takes a lot of confidence to be a test pilot, to expand the limits of aviation knowledge, to enter the unknown areas of the sky which no one has ever entered before. So, in one of our discussions, I asked Sammy how he came about making the decision to attempt that first loop.

Here is his story. "Every morning, before reporting to the flight line, I prayed to GOD for guidance. Then I would attend two different meetings, each with engineers who had different recommendations, to discuss the day's flight schedule. The first group wanted me to attempt to do a loop in the helicopter. They assured me there would be no problem, all I had to do was point the nose down until I achieved an airspeed of 120 knots, then to pull back on the cyclic control to begin an upward climb and continue until the aircraft was upside down. They assured me that the rigid rotor system, unlike normal rotor systems, would continue to work even when upside down and allow me to safely complete a loop."

Sammy continued, "The second group advised me not to attempt to do a loop; they were afraid that the rotor system would not be able to handle the inverted flight, and I would crash to my death as so many had done before me.

"After the meetings, I would go to the flight line, climb into my gear, and walk out to the aircraft, all the time trying to decide what to do. Once in the air, I would shove the nose down, gain the airspeed, and haul back on the controls to initiate a loop. As the aircraft arrived at the point just prior to inverted flight, I would kick the rudder pedal, and terminate the attempt."

"This happened every day for a while, and each day I would pray to GOD for direction. Finally one day, as I prayed while the aircraft was in a dive getting ready to start the loop attempt, I felt GOD answer me in a still voice that I could successfully complete the loop. At that point, I held the cyclic in my stomach, and rode the aircraft upside down, and on around to complete the loop. I did it with a mysterious sense of peace because of that answer."

Sammy's words gave more meaning to the term, "GOD is my Co-Pilot." He was a brave pilot who listened to his co-pilot as he explored the skies, testing the limits of both his aircraft and his belief.

Chuck Tucker and I after our first night flight.

The Hung-up Beta Control

Reprint from VERTICAL WORLD magazine.

It was another picture perfect day in Oxnard, California at the Lockheed California flight test facility. My flight test engineer and I were in the cockpit of the AH-56A gunship on a test flight. The Cheyenne was a revolutionary compound helicopter that was beyond the current state of the art. Unlike any other helicopter, it possessed a rigid rotor system that gave it great stability in the air and allowed it to achieve over 250 knots in straight and level flight.

The ship had wings that generated lift above a certain airspeed, at which point the pilot could reduce the main rotor blades to a flat pitch, and the aircraft would then fly like an airplane rather than a helicopter. For forward propulsion, it utilized a 10-foot diameter pusher prop that was controlled by a throttle on the collective, which operated like a motorcycle grip. It was called the beta, and the pilot controlled the aircraft's speed by rotating the grip and changing the pitch in the pusher, or beta, prop.

I was a happy guy! Lockheed was actually paying me to fly this incredible machine. On this particular morning, my flight test engineer and I were doing some speed tests. We were at about 4,000 feet and ready to go to the next point. I rotated the beta to the forward stop, to get the aircraft up to speed quickly. When we arrived at the test speed, I tried to rotate the beta backward to slow the aircraft down again, but it wouldn't move. The beta was stuck, and I couldn't break it loose.

Now we had a problem: How do we land an aircraft that cannot be slowed down? It would be like trying to park a car with the throttle wide open. The runway at Oxnard was not very long, and the brakes on the Cheyenne were not designed for this kind of situation.

The flight test staff made the decision to try a standard helicopter approach: nose high, with a big flare at the bottom to kill off the airspeed. Then, level off, touchdown, kill the engine and apply the brakes. It sounded good to me, and on the approach, I did manage to reduce the airspeed as planned. But when I dropped the nose to level off, the aircraft began to accelerate, and I knew I could never stop before I ran into the fence at the end of the runway.

I pulled back on the cyclic and initiated a climb-out back up to altitude. Leveling off once again at 4,000 feet, we began reconsidering our options. We were in a runaway aircraft with no ejection seat. We considered killing the engine and auto-rotating, but the auto-rotating characteristics of the Cheyenne with that big wing ruled out that option.

I decided I had to break the beta control loose from whatever had jammed it. However, my position in the cockpit did not allow me the leverage to exert much pressure on it. I unbuckled my seat and parachute harness, shoved the collective to the floor, and twisted around in the cockpit so that I could bring both hands to bear on the beta control. Twisting as hard as I could, with a lot of grunting and straining, and ignoring the fact that the aircraft was rapidly losing altitude, I felt the beta finally break loose. I very quickly twisted back around, regained control of the ship, buckled myself back in, and began my approach back to the Oxnard runway where I made a normal landing. The crash trucks and fire trucks standing by all returned to their stations, and we all heaved a big sigh of relief that was no doubt heard around the area.

After testing, the engineers found the problem: a rubber gasket installed between the beta grip and the collective shaft broke when I rotated the grip. The rubber then bunched up to form a wedge that jammed the beta in the full-on position, and made it too hard for me to break it free with only my left hand.

The problem was nothing very technical, but it is those unknown kinds of things that make test flying interesting and so necessary for new and unproven aircraft.

The Night Fear Entered The Cockpit

It was a calm, balmy night flying over the Yuma Proving Grounds in Arizona as I sat in the front gunner's seat in the AH-56A Cheyenne helicopter gunship. The moon shown through the canopy, providing a bright clear nighttime view of the desert and our heliport below. My pilot, Chuck Tucker (who I called Chucker) and I were lining up on a night time gunnery run using the newly developed night vision system and our laser tracking device to test the accuracy of both. We were circling the heliport, waiting for the go-ahead from the flight test director to begin the test.

Finally we got the call; it was time to start our run. Chuck commenced a dive down to the tracking run, leveling off about 50 feet or so above the ground, speed about 200 knots, lining us up with the ground mounted target. We were right on track, and I found the target through the lens of my swiveling gunner's station and placed the pointer dead on target center. The Cheyenne was such a stable aircraft, Chuck had no problem keeping us on target as we zoomed down the track, successfully tracking the bulls eye the entire run. This was going to be a piece of cake.

As usual in flight testing, things don't always go the way you want them to. As Chuck began his pullout at the completion of the run, suddenly we were both slammed down into our seats, but just as quickly thrown upward so hard our harness was forced into our shoulder blades, then down again, and up again, rapidly bouncing up and down in a terrible vibration so hard we couldn't focus our eyeballs. Then, just as quickly, it smoothed out.

Everything was quiet as Chuck continued his climb back to altitude and said, "What the **** was that?"

We were both afraid of what it could have been, a condition that was called "half P hop," where the aircraft begins a series of intense vibrations. This happened to one of our test pilots, David Beal, and the aircraft literally disintegrated around him and resulted in his death. The Lockheed engineers felt that after extensive research including work done in the Ames wind tunnel, that the cause had been found and corrected.

The word came from the Flight Test Director to climb and maintain altitude. No other comments after that terrifying incident which left both Chuck and I wondering what was going to happen next.

Chuck asked me, "Do you think they'll ask us to do that run again?" I was looking down at the heliport and could see all the activity going on; you could tell they were getting ready for something important, but still nothing from the Test Director. "Yes," I finally replied, "Tonight Chuck we find out how big our **** are."

Sure enough, the call we both expected and dreaded came to repeat that last run. It was stated in a very calm, quiet voice, as if everything had been normal. Of course, for us, sitting in the cockpit getting ready to risk our lives, it was anything but normal.

Chuck and I both let out a big sigh of resignation as he began the descent back down to the tracking run. As we neared the beginning of the run, we both felt that this could be our final flight. I decided that I would make this the best tracking run I had ever done.

We were on the track, the target dead ahead, 50 feet off the ground at night. The target was centered in my eye piece growing larger as we approached at 200 knots as I concentrated on the tracking to keep my mind off what would happen when Chuck begins his pull out and the dreadful vibrations that would follow.

This is it; Moment of truth! Time to pull up! Chuck eased the cyclic back to begin our climb out as we both held our breath in anticipation. Nothing happened. The Cheyenne was her normal smooth self, and we climbed back up to altitude and began our circle over the air dome, waiting for further instructions from flight test.

Chuck asked, "Do you think they'll ask us to do it again?" I sat there, looking at the full moon shining through the canopy, wondering what I was doing here and why I had been spared. Then I thought of my home, wife, and two sons and realized I really didn't want to be here anymore. I answered Chuck, "They don't have the right to ask us to do it again."

Finally the call came from flight test, "Okay guys, let's go home." Chuck banked over and began our descent to the heliport, anxious to get out of the cockpit and safely on the ground again.

It was still a balmy night, but now even more beautiful, because we were still alive!

The Death Of A Test Pilot

It was early in the morning when I stepped off the DC-3 aircraft that had flown me to the Lockheed Flight Test facility in Oxnard, California. Waiting for me was my fellow pilot, David Beal. David and I drove into Oxnard to have breakfast together while the engineers and mechanics got their ships ready for the first flight of the day.

David was an ex-Navy fighter pilot who had gone through the Navy test pilot school. He was assigned lead pilot on the envelope expansion ship for the Cheyenne test program. This is the most critical of the test pilot positions, since this aircraft is the one that has to explore and determine exactly how fast, far, and high the aircraft will perform. The engineers and designers work very hard to determine those limits on paper, but it is the flight test program that actually determines the final results. A new aircraft sitting on the ramp has a very small envelope. It is the test pilot's job to push the aircraft faster and higher, expanding its envelope, while exploring the unknown qualities of a particular design. And sometimes, the test pilot pays the ultimate price for that exploration.

Our morning breakfast gave us an opportunity to get to know each other better, talking about families, desires, and our job. We both loved to fly, and since we were young, we felt that we were invincible and had no fear of our jobs. It was just another flying job, better than most since we were flying state-of-the-art aircraft, designed and built by a leading aircraft manufacturer. The same aircraft company that produced such aircraft as the famous WWII fighter, the P-38 and the first operational jet fighter, the P-80. And out of the skunk works came aircraft like the U-2 and SR-71, the big black bird. Yes, we were proud to be test pilots for a company with that reputation.

We talked about mundane things. One of the things David told me that he missed was the opportunities to go snow skiing. The season was almost over and he had missed it due to the usual reasons, the work load and a new house with a new child. He had recently purchased a new house for his family, and still had a lot of work to do to make it the way they wanted.

We also talked about flying the Cheyenne. It was such an exciting aircraft; you picked it off the ground like a helicopter, but once you applied the power, it flew like an airplane. You had the best of both worlds. We also recognized that the rigid rotor system the aircraft utilized would bring the helicopter to the forefront of aviation, and we were the guys who were going to bring it there.

So you can see why we looked forward to our breakfast meetings together. We were also competitive and each tried to get our ship out the gate to the taxiway, egging crews to complete the checks so we could beat the other to take off.

On this particular morning, Dave pulled out just in front of me, and the two ships taxied out nose to tail, with me staring at Dave's big 10-foot diameter Beta pusher prop. Dave took off and headed for the coast line for his test runs while I lifted off with a flight test engineer in the front seat, and headed off for an avionics test over the valley.

My flight that day was for almost two hours before we headed back to the airfield. When we landed, I looked around and didn't see Dave's ship anywhere. Because of the type of experimental tests he did, his flights were of a short duration. Climbing out of the cockpit, I walked over to the carryall (SUV) that his group of engineers sat in during his flights. That way when there was a problem, Dave could radio the carryall and talk to the engineers about the problem and possible solutions. They were all very gloomy looking, so I asked where David was. They looked at me and said, "We have a problem." I asked, "What do you mean? David should have been back by now. What's happened?" They didn't know, and had not heard from him. The chase plane reported that he had gone down.

I was dispatched in a regular helicopter to go over his flight path to see if I could find anything. All I found were pieces of his aircraft floating in the water close to shore. His aircraft had experienced an unusual and unknown vibration so severe that the rotor blades began

119

flapping and went through the canopy, killing David instantly. The aircraft then started to come apart in midair, scattering pieces all over the coast line. I went into the hanger when I landed. The engineers were all looking down at their drawings, and the secretaries were all crying; no one knew what to do.

Our chief pilot, Ray Goudy, called me into the pilots' lounge and told me to go home. We were grounded until the engineers could figure out what had gone wrong, and how to correct it before we would fly again.

That night when I arrived at my home, I told my wife, "Pack your bags, tomorrow we're going snow skiing" I realized then that you can't put off things in life that you want to do, for you never know how much life you have left to accomplish it.

Dave was the only pilot killed on our program, but another pilot, Chuck Hench, was killed testing aircraft for another company after our program was completed. I used to play ping-pong with Chuck in the hanger at Yuma Proving Grounds during our lunch breaks. I could never beat him. This picture of him and me was taken just before one of our flights together.

The Day The Designers And Builders Of The Cheyenne Saw It Up Close

I got called back to the plant at Van Nuys to ferry a Cheyenne back to the flight test facility at Oxnard. The ship had just come out of an inspection, and I was selected to take it up and check it out. I waited in our flight shack for the flight test engineer in charge, Bill Groth, to come get me when the ship was ready.

After a long wait, Bill came and said the ship was ready, and it was time to go. Then he did something which was a little uncommon for Bill; he picked up my helmet and carried it out for me. As we walked out the door, I was shocked because the ramp was full of people. They were all standing behind a rope stretched across the ramp across from the Cheyenne.

It was very quiet as they were all looking intently at the aircraft. I asked Bill what was going on. He said that all the personnel on the Cheyenne project had requested to come out and watch the aircraft depart. I realized that these were the people who had designed and built the various components of the aircraft, but seldom had an opportunity to see it all put together. This was an opportunity for them to see the complete package, and to take pride in their efforts.

I felt their eyes on Bill and me as we walked across the ramp and climbed aboard the aircraft. Bill was in the front seat, and I was in the rear pilot's seat. It was uncomfortable being stared at by all these people. They had worked on and designed individual pieces of this fine aircraft, and now it was my turn to take the finished product and demonstrate it for them. I had the honor of taking the result of their efforts into the air.

I was determined to make the best, smoothest lift off I could. Then I slowly rotated the aircraft to the right, then to the left so that they had a chance to see the entire aircraft. I even backed it up using the Beta prop and a few other maneuvers to demonstrate the capability of the ship. I felt the responsibility to do the best I could to show my appreciation of their efforts.

Finally it was time to go. I contacted the tower for permission to lift off directly from the ramp, and began a steep climb-out and departed the airfield, knowing that every eye in that group was fastened on the part of the aircraft that they had been involved with producing. That day I felt very proud to be a Lockheed Engineering Test Pilot.

Part VI
Sailing

Learning About Sailing

When I was flying one night with Los Angeles Airways, my Captain asked me if I had done any sailing. I replied, "You know, that's something I've always wanted to do, but never had the opportunity." He told me that he had a sailboat and asked if I would like to go sailing with him this weekend. I don't like to pass up opportunities, so I agreed to meet him.

I met him at the beach on Balboa Island with a six pack of beer, ready for a new adventure. My dream of a beautiful sailboat was quickly shattered as he was standing next to a 7-foot boat, a dinghy with a sail. It wasn't quite what I had in mind, but I was ready to give it a try. Straddling the mast, I climbed into the boat as he pushed us off and began to adjust the sails; like magic, the boat began to move across the water. I fell in love. Men have been sailing across oceans for hundreds of years, but it was my first experience with moving across the water with only the wind for propulsion. No loud engine, no throttle control, actually very little control because to move a sailboat from point A to point B requires extensive knowledge of the rules of sailing.

But I was hooked. I went to the library and checked out everything I could find on sailing and began studying. I borrowed sailboats, sailboards, anything until I finally thought I knew enough to buy my own sailboat. It was a Venture 21, which was a trailable sailboat with a swing keel. But it had a small cabin on it, and would accommodate my family of four: myself, my wife, and two boys by this time.

The salesman brought me to the back bay of Newport to teach me how to raise the mast and rigging, how to get it off the trailer, and prepared me to begin sailing by myself. On our first weekend of ownership, we sailed under his supervision around the bay. The sails were sloppy, and I had a hard time adjusting the sails to the wind, but I got the boat out and then back again, and felt that I was ready.

The second weekend, I was ready for an adventure. I trailered the boat down to the docks at Long Beach with a plan to sail the 21-foot boat to Catalina Island, 26 miles away over open water. I thought it should be no problem. I was checked out, knew how to read a compass, and loaded my family and supplies for a weekend onto the boat sitting on the dock. I turned to another sailor and asked if he knew the compass heading to Avalon on Catalina Island. He told me and I proceeded to push off and begin the journey to an island, the one they sing about. Another dream of mine was going to come true.

Everything was great. A beautiful sunny day, a good steady wind, and the little boat was skipping across the waves. Being on the ocean was a much different experience after only sailing in protected waters. We were all settled in when the wind started dying down, and finally stopped altogether. No problem; I had a small outboard motor, an English seagull they called it, very primitive, but reliable, they told me. Sure enough, I got it started and we were now motoring our way to Avalon. Not as pretty with a noisy engine instead of the beautiful wing-filled sails, but we were making progress.

After motoring for quite a while, I realized it was going to take more fuel than I had to complete the trip, and wanted to make sure I saved enough fuel to pick up a mooring in Catalina, I shut down the engine. Now we were in the middle of the channel with no wind, and the sun was beating down on us. The family climbed into the cabin to get out of the sun, and we just sat there. I didn't know what to do at this point.

Then a big passenger carrying hydrofoil on its way to Avalon was coming in our direction. My wife insisted I try to contact them for help. My pride resisted, but she prevailed, and finally I began waving my arms to get the attention of the captain of the hydrofoil. He slowed down, his big boat settled back down into the water, and he began to circle my little sailboat. Using a speakerphone, he asked "Do you have any injured aboard?" I answered no, then he asked if we were in danger of sinking. Once again I answered no. So he asked, "Then what is your problem?"

I answered, "I'm out of fuel and there's no wind!" With that, he opened his throttles, the boat rose back up on his hydrofoils, and he replied, "Sail on the wind, sailor!" I yelled back a response which my wife did not approve of and fussed at me for using that kind of language. But he was right, I had no business out there with my family when I knew so little about sailing at that point. I went below, pulled out my sailing manual, and began to look for a solution to my problem.

We finally sailed into Avalon harbor late that evening before sunset, picked up a mooring, and spent the first of what would be many delightful trips in the future. I had learned my lesson, and many years later as I became more experienced, I purchased a much larger and seaworthy sailboat called the Cycona. It was a beautiful 26-foot Columbia which carried us many times to Catalina Island without the drama of that first trip.

But it was a valuable lesson which I learned the hard way.

The New Race Boat

It was a hot Wednesday afternoon, and my crew and I had just competed in a sail boat race at Marina Del Rey in my Columbia 26, a sailboat named the Cycona. We were relaxed, talking about the race, drinking beer, and just drifting along when one of the guys, Bailey Dotson, said "Hey, I know that guy in the Morgan sailboat!" So we motioned him over, and floated side by side in the marina while talking sailing. Finally, we asked him if he raced his Morgan, and he remarked he hadn't since he didn't have a crew. He needed 6 people to crew his boat in a race. So I said, "Well, I've got 3 guys, you've got 2, all we need is one more."

That was the start of our little group becoming sailboat racers. His name was Richard Cavalli, and his boat was a Morgan 36, really a good solid cruiser, stable, predictable, and not very fast. He eventually renamed the boat to a more fitting name for a race boat, after the singer Bob Marley, and it became Jammin! We raced Jammin for a couple of years, partied a lot, had some good times, but didn't win any races. Along the way, we became pretty good sailors for a bunch of businessmen who didn't begin sailing until their 30's.

One day Richard called to tell us he had purchased a new sailboat, and we should go down to the marina to check it out. We asked how to find it, and he said to look for the tallest mast. The name of the boat was SHOCKWAVE; it had a blue hull with a white deck. He gave us the pier and slip number to find it.

Well, we found it. It was a beautiful boat, state-of-the-art design and built with modern advanced materials. She was a pure race boat, not a converted cruiser. The equivalent of a formula 1 race car. It was built in Auckland, New Zealand and was known around the boating world as a class winner. It raced in what was called the IORA class, or International Offshore Racer, Class A. This was no weekend cruiser, but an out-and-out racing machine. There was no kitchen, no head (bathroom), and only a single burner propane stove to heat coffee, but there were bags and bags of sails up forward.

128

We walked all over the deck in awe, amazed at the size of the wenches which were twice as big as we were used to. Down below, we found at least 13 bags of sails, each sail good for only a limited amount of wind speed. That meant a lot of sail changes while racing. In addition, there was a computer for general navigation and to help locate the racing marks in the ocean. There were six bunks for sleeping, a portable head, and an ice box for the beer, but no cabin. Also, bulk heads were placed throughout the hull for strength, with open space from the stern all the way to the bow, a stripped down ocean racer!

It also required more crew. We could not race the boat with less than 13 crewmen. Finding them was no problem as everywhere we went, we were greeted by some sailor yelling, "Hey mate, need some crew?" The boat was well known and respected, so we soon had a whole contingent of Australian and New Zealander crewmembers. And these guys were good! Most had begun sailing at a very young age, while we original members were late bloomers. They had forgotten more than we ever knew about competitive sailing.

The boat was fast, so we were now in the big leagues. Sometimes while out practicing, an America Cup boat would pull alongside and ask to practice against us. That meant we were competing at one level below the top class in the world. And we sailed hard! Lee rail buried in the water, heeling over so far it was hard to move around on deck, constantly trimming sails, sails going up, and sails going down as the wind changed, bow smashing through the waves, sending spray all the way down the length of the boat. It was a constant rush!

The stress began to take its toll. One by one, members of the original crew began to drop out. The companies that designed and manufactured the sails provided expert personnel to trim the sails. Then the skipper brought an Olympic sailing champion for strategy, another to take over the helm, football players to grind the wenches, and so on. One of the guys couldn't scramble across the pitching deck because of his weight, another wasn't strong enough to grind the winches as we sailed harder and harder all the time. I was the last of the original crew because I knew how to operate the onboard computer. But inevitably, the time came for me to abandon the computer to a real expert as SHOCKWAVE became more competitive in southern California sailing circles.

But it was fun while it lasted. We learned a lot about sailing from the experienced guys who were of such an advanced caliber. We raced down to Mexico, around Catalina Island, practiced sail changes every Wednesday, and raced every other weekend. We spent a lot of time on the water. We were all proud to say that we had been part of the crew of SHOCKWAVE, one of the fastest sailboats in southern California.

A Sea Story

It was a nice, sunny day in southern California, a great day to go sailing. I belonged to an association of owners of Columbia 26 sailboats. We had planned a cruise down the coast to the harbor at Redondo Beach to spend a day at the yacht club there before sailing back up to Marina Del Rey. We had 6 boats in the group and joining my family on our boat, Cycona, we had Richard and Linda Glen-Davies and their two sons. All 8 of us climbed onto the 26 foot sloop and began to store our gear and food, which was a lot because half of the crew were young boys who constantly ate. We finally got everything stored and pulled away from the dock to join up with the other boats in the group.

The trip down was uneventful, lots of talking, eating, shared companionship between ourselves and the other boats. The sun was reflecting off the ocean as we sailed down the coast on a gentle broad reach. Everyone got a chance at steering the boat, and feeling the ocean slip underneath us as we lazily sailed along.

Our friends, the Glen-Davies, had sailed with us before, and we knew them to be fun, relaxed people who enjoyed adventures with their family. However, they didn't expect the day to bring the excitement which followed.

All the boats tied up at the guest docks in the Redondo Marina, and we went ashore for dining, drinking, and socializing. It was a good day, and for us, the excitement of exploring a different marina in a group was a real pleasure.

We were having so much fun we stayed longer than planned, and were one of the last boats to pull away from the guests' dock. The sun was sinking below the horizon to the west. Without checking the weather, which at times in southern California was a waste of time, we confidently rounded the breakwater on our way back to Marina Del Rey.

Sitting in the cockpit of a well found sailboat, surrounded by a loving family and friends after a nice day together is one of the best feelings in the world, and I felt quite content. But I kept noticing a change in the weather, a line of dark clouds was forming on the horizon to the west, and seemed to be coming closer at an alarming rate. I became concerned, and started to consider my options.

Meanwhile, the rest of the fleet continued toward home, with all the skippers keeping a wary eye on the approaching clouds. Finally I realized this was a serious storm and some action had to be taken. A sailboat is a very reliable craft, but 8 people on a 26-foot boat was a big responsibility.

I called for my foul weather gear, and we began preparing for a blow. I reduced the sails, and started up the engine. The wave action was steadily increasing as we motored along. I realized I had forgotten to release the cable supporting the boom from the aft stay. Everyone went below and closed the hatch while I tied myself in. Then we were hit broadside by a tremendous gust of wind which caused the boat to heel over and bury the lee rail. It was immediately followed by a strong, steady, howling wind and large waves.

I turned into the waves to keep from rolling over and called for Richard to help me lower the sails completely. We fought the sail down and tied it off, but it was a wild, wet struggle. Some of the boats continued to Del Rey, but I decided that since we were not yet to the half way point of the distance, and with two precious families aboard, the best course of action was to return to Redondo.

Richard went below and saw what a wild ride we were having, and how frightened everyone was. I was alone topside tied to the lifelines, and working the waves as best I could to maintain our course and yet try and reduce the wave action for the comfort level of everyone below.

It was at this point that a great talent of Richard's came forth. He began telling stories to the boys and their mothers. They became so enthralled that they were soon ignoring the tossing of the boat and the noise of the wind and waves. I would take a peek through the small opening in the hatch and was amazed at their rapt attention to his stories. Outside, I was creating my own story. Finally, the breakwater was in sight, but we were not home free yet.

Waves were breaking along the rocks off the entrance of the marina, making the approach very tricky and dangerous. It was going to require some good timing to successfully gain entrance.

The waves seemed huge, the night was very black, the wind was howling, and the sound of the waves breaking on the rocks made me have to yell to make myself heard. I wanted to catch the front of an approaching wave and ride it into the harbor. Finally, the wave I was looking for arrived, and we almost surfed into the harbor on the front of that wave. A sharp turn to the left put me behind the breakwater, and the water was thankfully calm.

Finding an empty slip, we tied up, and then I realized how frightened I had been. We spent the night on the boat using blankets provided by friends in the marina. It was a little crowded, but snug and secure after our wild ride.

I was proud of that boat, the Cycona, the design and construction which allowed us to safely return to a safe harbor. It took me a long time to finally go to sleep. I had to reassure myself about ten times that my friends and loved one were all safe, and I should not ever again trust the weather around the California coast.

The Old Man And The Young Boat

Here I am, your average over 40 sailor who likes to drink beer and have a good time, crewing on an outdated sailboat. We wanted to race, but not too seriously, drink beer, have a good time, and maybe occasionally win a trophy. Along the way, almost by accident, we got pretty good and had visions of crewing on a really hot boat. Dreams of taking part in a TransPac, Mexico, SORC, and all that good stuff.

Then our skipper finally went out and really did it! He bought a new boat. But what a boat! One of the top IOR (International Offshore Racer) racers in the country. We were awestruck when we took her out for the first time. This was no weekend warrior, this was the real deal!

The boat required more crew. It was too much boat for just six guys to handle, as good as we thought we were. It needed eleven men to handle this hot-rod. So, who do we get? ROCK STARS! You've seen them around marinas, I mean these guys are good. None of the original six of us had even started sailing until we were in our thirties. We were too busy raising and paying for families. These guys began sailing around the age of six, and they had a long list of impressive sailing accomplishments.

So here we were, on a hot-rod of a boat, surrounded by rock star sailors, the level of challenging skyrockets. The intensity was immense. No more trim a little here and then a little more there and pass up another beer. Now it was constant attention, looking always for more speed.

The moment comes when we all face our limitations. On the old boat, we were all young and in much better shape than your average 40 year olds. But now it was different. That dreadful moment arrives when you can't grind anymore and have to move aside and watch a young man spin the winch. Or, your back is killing you on the halyard, and a pair of strong arms come to your assistance. And in the middle of the night, sitting on the weather rail, three pairs of socks, foul weather gear over layers of clothes, you begin to wonder why you're freezing out here instead of snuggled in that warm bed.

But then, thankfully, dawn comes, and the sun begins to warm your bones. The boat is leaping almost playfully across the waves, a beautiful responsive boat filling you with the sense of being alive, or being in touch with the natural flow of the earth and sea, and once again, we're young.

Living On A Boat In Marina Del Rey

A lot of guys dream of living on a boat, but women, not so many. However, the reality of living on a boat is quite different from the dream. First of all, they are small. Then, they are damp. And they are in constant motion, even at the dock. They require a lot of upkeep, especially a beautiful wooden boat. You don't have a lot of storage space, and everything has to be in its place, so you learn to live very simply and neatly, no need for anything extra.

I lived on a boat for a couple of years, and loved it. It was a 37' yacht built by the Egg Harbor Company, a Cadillac of boats type of company. It had twin engines down below, a spacious aft cabin with a queen bed, a full galley, (kitchen for the unwashed??) a head (bathroom) which included a shower, all the comforts of home. Plus it was a wooden boat, with beautiful lines including a flying bridge. It was named GLORY, and I had it moored in Marina del Rey.

I'll never forget my first night on the boat. I put brand new cotton sheets on the bed, climbed into my pajamas, and didn't sleep all night. It was too cold. The covers didn't help, and extra clothes made no different either. It was just too cold.

The next morning as I climbed out of the boat to go to the shoreside bathroom, some dock mates living on a boat nearby asked me how my night went. They started laughing as I told them of my miserable night. They told me to take off those cotton sheets and put some flannel sheets on my bed and that would solve my problem. I took their advice, and sure enough, the flannel sheets gave me a good night's sleep. It seems that cotton absorbs the dampness and never warms up, while the flannel sheets don't, and they allow for a nice warm sleep. I've been sleeping on flannel sheets ever since, even in warm Louisiana.

People used to comment on how cheerful and fresh I looked on some mornings, but I had a secret. Sometimes I would wake up early in the morning when everyone else was sound asleep. I would get dressed, go out and untie the ship from the dock. Climbing on the bridge, I would crank up the engines, and slowly back out of my slip and head into the marina and out the breakwater to the open ocean. I would power out about a mile from the beach, into the smooth water, and kill the engines. Next I would drop deck lines into the water on the starboard side and the stern. Finally, I would take off all my clothes, dive off the bow of the boat and swim around to the stern where I pulled myself aboard again. Then I would repeat this two or three more times before drying off, getting dressed, and heading back to the marina. It was very refreshing, and exciting. I threw the deck lines off the side of the boat in case I spotted some sharks and had to get back on board quickly, without having to swim all around to the stern. That was my early morning wake up routine.

In my years sailing, I've seen sharks, and they are evil looking creatures. Fortunately I see only their fins as I do not want to be in water around sharks. I did have a very scary incident on a trip to Catalina Island with a good friend of mine, Rod Roddewig. Rod and I sailed my sailboat, a Columbia 26 to spend a weekend in Avalon, the village on the island. It's a beautiful tranquil beach town, very scenic, with good restaurants. We were both single at the time and wanted a guy's get-away.

After the party was over, we boarded the boat and set sail for the long return trip to Marina del Rey. As we were sailing along, I looked out into the distance ahead of us and saw an unusual disturbance in the water. We pulled out the binoculars and discovered it was a band of black and white killer whales thrashing about. We watched them very carefully as they were on the path that we had to sail to make the point of the Palisades, that big point of land that sticks out into the Pacific south of Los Angeles. You don't have a lot of choice in selecting a course in a sailboat. The path you take to get someplace is totally dependent on the direction of the wind. And the wind dictated that that was the course we had to hold to make it around the point.

As we got closer to the whales, my friend Rod asked, "Isn't this dangerous?" "Yes," I replied, "but this is the course we have to take; if we turn away, it will take us hours to sail around the point."

Suddenly, we were upon them. If you've never seen a killer whale up close and personal, they are both beautiful and deadly at the same time. Rod pointed to the starboard side, and there was a big whale coming right at us, his eyes above the water as his nose was pushing a large wave in front of him, and I swear those eyes were looking right at me. At the last minute, he dove under our boat, and came up on the other side. Then he turned alongside our boat and swam next to us. We stood there stunned at his size. He was bigger than our boat. It really made us feel small. We were wondering if he was considering us for lunch.

What can we do?" Rod cried out. "Nothing," I replied. "We just hold our course and hope to sail out of their pack." And that's what we did; we just held the boat steady on track, made no sudden moves or noise, and quietly left those beautiful monsters playing in our wake. The rest of the trip back to the Marina del Rey was uneventful, but I'll never forget the look in the eyes of that killer whale as he swam toward us that afternoon off Catalina Island.

The Anchor Incident On Catalina Island

David Holmes and his wife Perry joined Marilyn and I for a cruise to Catalina Island. We were going to spend the weekend at anchor at the area called The Isthmus. The Isthmus was a favorite anchorage for sailors, protected from the wind and waves of the channel and lots of room to maneuver. It had a nice restaurant and bar, and not much of anything else ashore except a nice beach and shady palm trees. My friend, David was a good sailor, and one of the crew on the race boat, SHOCKWAVE so he knew what he was doing.

We sailed into the Isthmus and began looking for a good place to anchor with a lot of room to swing on our anchor without disturbing other boats. This is the normal practice, and anchoring is actually an art form. You don't just drop the anchor; you have to plan where to place it so it will hold, then back off and let the anchor line play out so the anchor will lie correctly on the bottom. This is called scope, and the rougher the water, the more anchor line you have to lay out. The idea is to have the line pull horizontally on the anchor, helping it to better grip on the ocean floor. When you enter a harbor like the Isthmus, finding a good place among all the other boats is not easy.

So we motored around the harbor, checking out different possibilities to drop anchor. We wanted to be fairly close to the shore line on the southern edge of the harbor, and to make sure we didn't drop our anchor line over anyone else's anchor line.

Finally we located a good spot, and went through the anchoring procedures to make sure it was going to hold. Then it was time to relax, fix a good rum and coke, and settle in with the ladies who had prepared some snacks for us to enjoy.

A few hours went by as we enjoyed the sun and just being there at such a beautiful location on my Columbia 26, the Cycona. We enjoyed watching other boats enter the harbor and go through the anchoring process, comparing their techniques, and laughing over some of their mistakes. It was a good day to be alive and safely anchored.

Then a sailboat of about 32 feet entered the harbor in sort of a rough fashion. It was crewed by two older gentlemen who looked as though they were beginners to sailing. They looked very confused as they searched for a good place to anchor. They pulled up next to us and asked if they could anchor there. We told them they were too close and needed to find another spot.

They kept motoring around like a couple of lost souls and were turned away from numerous other boats as well. Eventually, they returned close to us and proceeded to drop their anchor. As we had feared, they dropped their anchor so that their anchor line crossed over our anchor line. We yelled at them to pull up their anchor and move to another spot, but they ignored our pleas and went inside the cabin.

Now David is a quiet guy, hardly ever raises his voice, but quite a competent sailor (He actually saved me from losing my leg in a boating accident years later, but that's another story). After getting frustrated trying to get those two incompetent sailors to relocate their boat, David didn't say anything, but came out of the cabin holding a knife between his teeth. This was quite a picture; he looked like something out of a Tarzan movie, in swim trunks and holding a knife in his teeth. I started to ask what he was doing when he dove overboard and headed toward our wayward friends. As he neared the bow of their boat, he dove underwater and was gone from sight. Minutes later, our friends' boat began drifting backward as Dave surfaced with a grin on his face.

David had gone under and cut their anchor line. That finally got their attention, and they started scrambling, trying to decide what to do. They were yelling at us, but we all just stood there and enjoyed the Chinese fire drill taking place on their boat. Without an anchor, they had to start up their engine before they drifted onto the rocks which were getting closer every minute.

They finally got some control over their boat and motored away from us while yelling some choice words. We just stood there and gave them a fairwell salute and encouraged them to get out of our area. Once they had gone off trying to decide what to do, we decided it was time for another rum and coke to celebrate David's daring underwater adventure. No other boats attempted to anchor near us for the rest of the weekend.

Part VII
General Stories

The Miracle At Grand Coteau

Everyone called my father, JB, and I was called Berch. My full name is John Berchman Richard, Jr., but I never inquired where my name came from, and my parents never brought up the subject.

I knew a little of the history of my family on my father's side. Our ancestors were on the first boatload of Acadians to arrive in Louisiana. Their names are inscribed on a plaque placed behind the church next to the Evangeline Oak where they docked. There were two brothers, and they settled in a small village called Opelousas, Louisiana. Nearby was another small village called Grand Couteau where there was a school for nuns called the Convent of Sacred Heart.

In New London, Canada, a girl named Mary Wilson was born in 1846, and she wanted to become a nun. However, she was very sickly and eventually moved to south Louisiana in the hopes that the milder climate would be good for her health. Unfortunately, her health continued to decline until she found herself in the infirmary in the Sacred Heart convent in 1866. She was violently sick with a high fever and vomiting blood. From all indications, she would not live to gain the nunnery habit she desired. She prayed to John Berchmans, a Belgian priest who was being considered for saint hood. He was described as a very good, unassuming man. It takes three miracles to occur before a person can be ordained as a saint, and at this point, he had only two.

Finally, a priest was called in to perform the last rites over Miss Wilson, as she was not expected to live until morning. However, when the nuns arrived the next morning, Mary was perfectly healthy. They performed tests and found out all her health problems had gone. The nuns who first walked in and found her sitting up in bed were reported to have almost fainted. A miracle had occurred!

When they asked Mary what had happened, she said that she had prayed to John Berchmans, and if she didn't get better, she would no longer believe. A voice then told her to close her eyes and stick out her tongue. She obeyed, and something touched her tongue. The same voice said she was now healed, and would obtain her habit. She opened her eyes, but there was no one there.

As a result of this miracle, John Berchmans was ordained a saint, the only saint to be ordained in the United States.

My parents passed away before I knew any of this history. My sister called me one day while I was in California and told me about an article she had read in the magazine LOUISIANA LIFE that told all about it. I flew to Louisiana, and drove to Grand Coteau. It was noontime on a Sunday. Everything was closed, but I searched all the buildings of the convent until I finally located an unlocked door. I went inside and located the infirmary where the miracle took place. It is now a shrine to St. John Berchmans. Continuing to explore, I discovered a very old large book in the entryway. It was hand-written, and told the whole story of the Miracle of Grand Coteau. I stood there in the gloom and read the entire account. It sent shivers up and down my spine.

My father, like so many other Catholic men in that part of Louisiana, was named after this miracle, and my father passed that blessing on to me. So if you come into contact with a man with the name of Berchman, you know his heritage is from the deep Cajun country around Grand Coteau, Louisiana, and he is blessed.

The Football Player

In my ninth grade year, I went out for football even though at the time I only weighed 120 pounds soaking wet. I worked out hard since I wanted to earn a jersey. The day finally came when our coach decided who would and who wouldn't receive a jersey. I sat there on pens and needles as one boy after another received the coveted purple and white jersey. Finally, the jersey box was almost empty, and still, I sat there. The coach reached in, pulled out the last jersey, and called my name. You would have thought I had just won a grand prize due to my elation over having received the jersey. I had made the team. But at the end of the season, I knew that football wasn't for me. Especially after the following experience.

I had the jersey, and dressed out with the rest of the team, but the coach never gave me a chance to play. I was desperate for the coach to give me a chance. I was small, but I couldn't run fast because of having polio as a child. The after-effect of the polio had restricted movement of my right leg, so I was confined to playing in the line where all the biggest guys played.

About that time, we had an Air Force neighbor who was a big guy and had played Canadian football in his younger days. I told him of my situation, and he offered to show me a few plays to get past a bigger player. What a gift; it was just the opportunity I needed to show the coach what a small guy like me could do with the proper training. My big friend worked with me until I had the moves down pat. He taught me three techniques that would allow me to get past my opponent and make a tackle on a running back behind the line of scrimmage. I couldn't wait to go to the next practice to show what I had learned.

Practice came, but I was sitting on the sidelines, hoping for a chance to go in. I asked a friend named Blackie to let me go in at his position. He was playing second string guard, and that was where I needed to be to use my tricks. Blackie kept putting me off, but finally called me and said, "Hey Berch, still want to come in?" I of course said yes, and trotted onto the field, ready to show my stuff. What I didn't know was that the coach had put the new guy, a giant by our standards, in the position opposite where Blackie had been playing, and Blackie had heard the switch. Blackie was no fool, and had let me come in and take his position against the new guy.

Imagine my surprise when the first team came out of the huddle, and the biggest guy on the field trotted up and settled in front of me. But that was okay; actually, it was even better, for now I could really demonstrate my fighting spirit to the coach. Talk about David and Goliath, it was the ancient matchup. But I wasn't worried; I was confident that I would show the coach and convince him to let me play more.

On the first play, I used one of my tricks, got past the giant, and caught the runner behind the line of scrimmage. You should have seen the look on the giant's face as he got into position for the next place. Again, I took advantage of my training, and actually caught the quarterback before he could complete his hand off. Now the giant was really upset; the smallest guy on the team was getting past him and making tackles. Once again, we settled into position, but I still had one more trick up my sleeve, and it worked again, catching the runner just as he received the hand off.

Boy was I feeling great! Still no notice from the coach, but I knew he was paying attention. Once again, we settled in for a play, but I was out of tricks, so knew I would have to repeat one. Now the giant was big, but he wasn't stupid. I tried a trick on him, but he was waiting for it, and he nailed me. Big Time! He tossed me up in the air, and I landed hard on my back, knocking the wind out of me. I couldn't get up; instead, I rolled over and called for Blackie to come back in. I had to crawl off the playing field. I was in terrible pain. The coach never said a word to me, absolutely no recognition of what I had accomplished. I knew then that to continue to play this game was a waste of my time. Sitting on the bench all season was not my idea of doing something worthwhile.

So, I decided to take a different route. I joined the marching band. They at least had girls on their bus trips, and that opened up more possibilities for fun, without the bruises.

Evil In A Barn In South Louisiana

It was a beautiful summer day; we were young, healthy, and full of mischief. I was on a date with Sherry Lee, a vivacious pretty girl whom I admired. There was another couple with us. Sherry lived on the southern edge of Lake Charles, in a house next to a semi-deserted house occupied by a strange, old man who wasn't seen very much. We were in a playful mood, looking for things to do, when Sherry's girl friend said we should crawl over the fence and explore that old man's house.

It was a mysterious house, run-down, but with a lot of old farm equipment scattered over his big lot. It was not an inviting place, and it looked to offer excitement to four young teen-agers. We knew the old man was gone since his antique car was not in the yard, so we decided to take advantage of the situation.

We crawled over the fence and entered his house. It was not clean. In fact, it looked like it hadn't been cleaned in ages, but it had a lot of old, interesting items to explore. I came across a box of old Mechanics Illustrated magazines and became quite involved in reading them. Meanwhile, the girls were finding all sorts of things that kept them excited and exploring.

After a while, we wandered outside to look at the antique farm equipment he had; tractors, plows, that sort of thing. Eventually, we wound up going into the old barn to check it out. While looking around, the girls spotted a tassel hanging out of a big trunk. They had to know what it was attached to, so it was left up to the other boy and myself to climb up to the raised shelf to find out what it was.

Climbing up the old ladder, I walked over to the trunk and opened the lid. The trunk was packed tightly with old clothes, and the tassel was buried under layers of old clothes. They were clean, but smelled musty, the smell of old, unused, long-packed clothes.

The girls kept demanding to see what the tassel was part of, so, being the brave adventurer, I took hold of the tassel and began pulling it out from under all the clothes packed over it. Finally I gave a big pull upward, and it came loose. I had it completely out, the rest of the tassel in the sunshine in probably the first time in many years. The girls let out a sudden gasp, and I felt the atmosphere in the barn change. It was no longer a charming old barn, but had become something evil, for the tassel was connected to a red silk hood of a KKK leader. I am not sure how it happened, but that red, evil-looking hood reeked of evil. You could tell it had been a witness or even a participant to things that were against human nature.

Then, while we were all standing there captured by the sight of that red silk hood, we heard the sound of a car entering the gravel driveway. The old man was coming home! I quickly jammed the hood back under the clothes, dropped the trunk lid back down, and literally jumped down from that shelf. Then we all headed out the door and to Sherry's house, making sure to keep his house between us we crawled over his fence and made a mad dash for the kitchen door and safety.

We never went over to the old man's house again. It was no longer a thing of curiosity, but rather a place of evil to be avoided. I've never forgotten that red silk hood, and the smell of evil that came from it.

The House Builders

When my Dad, JB, bought the house on Alamo Street in Lake Charles in the late 40s, he must have had some grand plans for it since it included a big empty lot adjacent to it. For a long time, that lot served as a recreation area for my friends and me. Unfortunately, it was also a big job for me to have to cut the grass on that lot, especially since lawn mowers were push mowers in that day. You had to push them by hand, and the difficulty was increased as the grass grew taller. This taught me the lesson of not putting off undesirable jobs, but getting them done while they are still relatively easy. The grassy area was soft and tended to get muddy when we were playing football on it, and we got muddy as well. We would slip and slide all over that yard, trying to maintain some resemblance to an actual football game. It was great fun, but our mothers hated it.

One day my father decided to build a little rent house on the back part of that yard, where Mother used to have her clothesline. We had no plans or blueprints; we just got started. Dad got a level, and we laid the foundation using string and a water hose filled with water. It was very primitive stuff, but it worked. We laid the floor beams atop concrete pillars, then nailed the subfloor. We even did the plumbing, packing the pipes, and digging the ditches. I never liked plumbing after that, and neither did my father. It was all hard, slow work with just the two of us after he got off work every day.

Every day, as soon as Dad got home from the refinery, my mother had coffee waiting for us, and we got to work. We would work until it got dark before going in for dinner. If there was work to do inside the house, we would continue after dinner. It seemed to take forever. I asked Dad to let me paint the house on a contract basis, and he agreed. He gave me a set amount to do the complete job including paint and supplies. He was used to using paint brushes and was surprised when I came up with these new-fangled gadgets called paint rollers. He didn't think much of it until he saw the results, and was pleased. After that, I painted all the interiors, and some of the exteriors of all the houses we built, for our house building era was just beginning.

Finally, the house was finished, and rented. Later on, it became the first house that my sister, JoAnn, and her husband lived in as a married couple. The house was a good investment and paid for itself.

Then one day, Dad looked at the big empty lot, my playing field, and said, "Let's build a duplex on this lot." I got really upset, remembering all those long nights and spoiled weekends building that small house. What was this going to be like? It wasn't any fun. First the lot had to be leveled, one shovelful at a time. None of that fancy earth moving equipment for my Dad, just he and I every afternoon, shoveling dirt to level the lot. He had a huge pile of dirt delivered to the yard, and every afternoon after school, I would go outside, take off my shirt and begin shoveling dirt into a wheelbarrow, then dumping the load in a low spot. I did this over and over again, until the lot was ready to begin building. This routine played an important role in my first brush with the law while I was in high school, and I learned a lot more respect for my father. Following is the story of that incident.

I used to drive my future wife to school every day in my 1935 three window Ford coupe. But one day, she was sick and had to stay home. When I arrived at LaGrange Sr. High School in Lake Charles, some of my buddies suggested we play hooky and drive to Orange, Texas. Always ready for adventure, we piled into three cars, including my friends, John Sorrells and Monte Hurley, and took off. We arrived in Orange around noon, and hung around the street outside of the local high school, talking tough and acting tough, while scared to death we would get caught. One of my buddies had the great idea of placing rubber hose over my exhaust pipes with Popsicle sticks to make them extremely loud, a trick he had learned somewhere. Sure enough, when I cranked the little V-8 up, it was so loud it hurt our eardrums. We all jumped in and took off, but too late, for a police car pulled up in front of us and stopped us. As a result, we were placed in jail.

We all called our fathers, and most received a tongue lashing. But my father asked what charges we were being held on, and if there were none, he demanded we be released immediately. All of the other fathers made no such demand, but we were all turned loose. Some of the fathers told their sons they would come and get them, or to ride with other fathers back home. My father told the police if his son had his own car, he could drive back home by himself.

When I got home, my mother did not say a word. While I put on my work clothes, she fixed me a cup of coffee and I took it outside to begin shoveling dirt to level out the yard for construction. I felt pretty bad; my mother was pregnant, but never said a word. Finally, my father arrived home from work. He got his coffee, changed into his overalls, and came outside to join me. He never said a word; just started shoveling dirt next to me. After a while, we took a break, and leaning on his shovel, he asked me, "Well son, did you learn a lesson today?" "Yes Sir," I replied. But the real lesson I learned that day was that my quiet father was a brave, real man, and no one was to trifle with his son. I was very proud of him.

Finally, after what seemed to take forever, the duplex was completed, and now my Dad had three rental units available. All of them were built with the sweat, literally, of our brows. However, this time, Dad decided to have someone else do the plumbing and electrical. We just did the hammering, cutting, painting, roofing, and all the other thousand details that go into house building.

When I told Dad that I wanted to get married, being a practical man he asked, "Where do you plan on living?" Being a romantic man, I hadn't even considered it. He said he had always wanted to tear down the old garage/workshop and build a garage apartment there. If I helped him build it, my wife and I could live in it as long as we wanted for only the cost of the loan payment. It seemed like a good idea, and I agreed.

It was a good idea as well as a good experience. It really helped to bind my future bride and myself as it gave us actual opportunities to fulfill our dreams of designing our own living quarters. Once again, true to our style, we had no plans; we just built as we went along. First, we tore down the old garage. That was the fun part. Next, Dad contracted for someone to erect the bottom floor of concrete blocks, which contained a two-car garage and a wash room. When that was completed, we went into action. Dad and I laid in the subfloor and then decided it was time to figure out the floor plan. Marilyn, my future bride, my Dad and I climbed up the ladder and walked around the subfloor, trying to decide where we wanted the walls, doors, windows, and that kind of stuff. We walked around, nailing a 2x4 here, another one there, to designate where a wall was to be erected later.

While we were laying out the bathroom, I laid a board down showing Marilyn where the wall was going to be and asked her if she agreed with that location. I also asked if it was big enough since she had grown up in a house where the bathroom was so cramped that when you sat on the commode, your knees were up against the bathtub. She said, "I've always wanted a big bathroom; could you make it bigger?" Anxious to please, I pulled up that board, moved it a couple of more inches and asked, "Is this big enough?" She smiled and that was both my answer and reward, and that was where the wall was built. It was probably the biggest bathroom in such a small apartment you will ever see.

The marriage date was set to allow for completion of the apartment. We had our own home to come back to after the honeymoon. We lived there for over three years while I went to college; fortunately, we never had to live with either of our parents. It was good to know that the first home you lived in as a married man, you had built with your own hands. Not many men can say that in today's world.

All those units are still standing as a testimony to my father's skill and industry.

My wife, Marilyn, in the window of the apartment Dad and I built.

The Little Cajun Goes Snow Skiing

My flying days were over, and I was looking for a new career. It had to be an outdoor type of job; no office job for me. Also, I wanted something that was good for mankind. No more testing of war machines. It was fun blasting away at targets from a fast moving armed helicopter, but I felt it was time to go in another direction.

My partner and I attended a seminar which offered all sorts of franchises and opportunities for budding businessmen like ourselves. We got involved with a company that made a product called Bike Banks. It was a coin-operated bicycle locking rack that used a patented locking mechanism. We had visions of placing these racks at all the college campuses in California and spending our working days on college campuses and bike paths collecting quarters.

We put out a lot racks on major college campuses as planned, and even got a contract to install them on the Venice, California bike path. We were collecting quarters, but not in the amount that was sufficient to feed two families.

Trying to find more product to produce income, we visited the plant where the Bike Banks were made. While visiting their factory, I spied some long boxes stacked against the rear wall of their shop. They told me the boxes contained Ski Banks, using the same locking mechanism as the Bike Banks, but were designed to be placed at ski resorts so skiers could lock their skis while taking a lunch break. Unfortunately, they told us the Ski Banks were too expensive for the resorts to purchase, and they had not developed a market for them. Doug and I discussed it, and made them an offer to purchase all their Ski Banks and spare parts. They were happy to get rid of them since they figured the market was already saturated.

We rented a truck and drove the Ski Banks to southern California, and that was the start of a brand new, successful business.

The units were painted an ugly black with white decals explaining the use, with poorly designed end frames to support the ten-foot

157

racks. At a party one night, I talked to a friend of mine named Skip VanLuen, who was a hot motorcycle racer in the flat track days.

He told me he was now in the snow ski apparel business and that skiers liked bright fashions. That made me decide to change the look of all those ski banks. I had them all sand blasted and repainted to a nice blue. I redesigned the supporting end frames and painted them red. Then I hired a graphic artist to design an attractive decal explaining how to use the ski racks.

That did the trick; with new brochures containing photos of our red, white, and blue racks just in time for the 1976 skiing season, Dan went to work peddling the racks to different mountain resorts in southern California.

Our plan was to sell one rack to a mountain, take the proceeds from that sale, build another one, and lend it to another mountain. We wanted to take advantage of the cash money stream that the racks generated. We were splitting the money with the mountain, so they did not have to lay out any money to buy one.

It was a good operation, and we were hand-building the racks in my garage. Then at another party, a good friend of mine, Richard Crosby, asked what I was doing. I told him about our ski rack program. Richard, a CPA, said that we were sitting on top of a great tax shelter program. We had no idea what a tax shelter was since we weren't in that income bracket, but we learned all about them pretty fast.

We located another partner who had money to invest, Joe Fryser, and we began a whole other operation. We expanded our operation, rented a warehouse in Chatsworth, California, and I began to set up a production line. No more building them one at a time with my own two hands.

Joe introduced us to an organization which was looking for a tax shelter program to sell to wealthy clients. Our plan was to sell a rack which held thirty-two locking stations to an investor. Then, as part of the sales price, we would locate his rack on a ski resort of his choice so that he could charge off all of his skiing expenses when he made a call to that mountain. We then shared the cash revenue that each rack provided with the mountain. That meant someone from our company would have to visit each ski resort, and accompanied by a ski resort employee, they would jointly collect the revenue from the ski racks. Normally, when our employees arrived to collect the revenue, they received guest ski passes, and spent at least one day skiing in addition to the days needed to collect and repair the ski racks.

The sales organization sold all the ski racks we could produce, and wanted more of that type of product to sell. So, we decided to make boot lockers. The metal shop that fabricated our racks were now told to make coin operated lockers. I had to come up with a design to allow our patented lock mechanism to be used in a vertical situation. That meant that a coin had to fall from the uppermost lock mechanism to the bottom of the locker and into the locking coin box. Once that was complete, we went into production for the lockers and once again, successfully located them on mountains using the same revenue-splitting program. We eventually located our equipment on 200 ski resorts around the country.

A wonderful bi-product of this business was, I got to ski on some of the finest ski mountains in the west, and became a pretty proficient skier. I've skied in Utah, Colorado, California, Arizona, and New Mexico. I've skied on hard packed, almost icy conditions, and soft, fluffy snow that was delightful. I've skied at fancy ski resorts and beginners' mountains. One particular ski resort in Arizona was operated by Indians, some in full costume. It was a seasonal business, and we always prayed for an early snow.

It was a very enjoyable and successful business while it lasted. Eventually, we were approached by a large company that offered to buy us out. They wanted to purchase the complete operation and have us to train their employees on the maintenance of the units located on the mountains, as well as introduce them to the resort managers.

We accepted their offer, and retired from the business. I continued to ski for a couple of more seasons, then began to look for another business to get involved with, and haven't snow skied since. I miss skiing, the beauty of the mountains, that cold, clean fresh air, the feeling of rushing down the mountain, while anticipating some hot chocolate by a roaring fireplace. It's a great sport, and one I never dreamed of as a young man growing up in south Louisiana.

Ultra Fun In An Ultralight

Today, October 14, 1990, I am introduced to a new adventure. At least it's new to me. I've flown small, single-engine planes, a little larger twin-engine plane, small bubble helicopters, and giant twin-engine passenger-carrying helicopters, not to mention a compound helicopter gun ship. But for flying fun, I've just found the answer. An ultra-light flying machine made by a company called. Quicksilver!

I was driving down this back road off the main highway in a place called Selma, Oregon. You know, just wandering around, exploring the area, looking for a reason for me to be there. While going around a corner, I noticed a flash of color to my right, and I spotted a hanger with some small planes outside. Finally, I found a gate which looked like it might lead me to the airfield. It opened onto a dirt road leading through the woods, and finally, there it was; an aircraft hangar, right in the middle of nowhere.

Flying around in an ultra-light has been described as flying in a lawn chair. They have the look of an updated version of the aircraft the Wright brothers flew at Kitty Hawk. The wings are covered with cloth, but a very modern, plastic-like cloth, and supported by wires and braces much like the old WWI flying machines. They have no fuselage to speak of, only a network of tubes and wires leading back to a fabric-covered tailpiece. Underneath the tailpiece is a real throw-back, a tail skid. Overall, it is a very unsubstantial piece of equipment.

But it looks like fun.

So, I made arrangements to fly one of them. I climbed in next to my instructor, an airline pilot who owns this little airfield. He briefed me on what we were going to do, how it flies, how it lands, and other valuable information. We crank the engine and begin to taxi to the far end of the grass strip. Turning into the wind, I apply the power to the small engine, and we begin to accelerate. It's quite a sensation, as there is nothing in front of you, no instrument panel, engine cowling, or windshield. There was just empty space and the grass rushing beneath your feet.

Now she gets light, and you can feel her wanting to leave the ground to become a thing of the air; this is the point where the strange and complicated contraption proves the value of the design. We lift off smoothly and begin to climb. To understand what it's like, imagine yourself sitting in your lawn chair, 200 feet in the air, moving along at record-breaking 40 mph. It is an incredible feeling of freedom. You are torn between the requirements of mastering this little flying machine and simply sitting back and enjoying the scenery. The earth is so beautiful when seen from above, the flowing of the streams, and the cultivated fields; it's all laid out so pretty for you.

Much like a sailboat on the ocean, the small flying ship is very sensitive to air currents. It simply rides and floats along, with no pretense of overcoming the air. You don't fly it to go to a specific location, for it doesn't have that freedom of purpose. You simply fly it for the pure pleasure of flight. And pleasure it does provide once you get comfortable and learn to sit back, relax, and enjoy it. At one point, just prior to turning on a crosswind for a landing approach, I spotted a bird flying on what appeared to be a collision course. For an instant I considered changing course, since I felt we were brothers, and I was new to the area. I had never had those feelings before. The sky was mine, and the bird had better get out of my way.

I continued my approach once the bird (my brother) changed his angle and lowered the nose (what nose? there isn't any, just my feet sticking out there in space). I pushed the stick forward and reduced power to begin the descent. Everything looked good until the last 75 feet. At that point, a thing called "ground rush" comes into effect. After slowly losing altitude for a couple of hundred feet, all of a sudden, the ground comes rushing up at you. Also, the wind has now come up, creating a cross-wind which wants to push the little craft, and me with it, off the centerline of the landing strip. The wings are rotating up and down, the ship is slipping sideways, and finally, I remembered how to handle a cross-wind. I drop the up-wind wing slightly and apply opposite rudder, and she straightens up nicely. Now to concentrate again on the ground which has made a lot of headway while I was trying to hold a straight course. I put a little back pressure on the stick, and she floats. Then, I ease back on the power, and she settles down and touches the ground.

Once again, we have returned to earth. The ship is again awkward, out of its element. I think both the ship and I want to once again become part of the sky, no destination in mind; actually no reason, except the exhilarating pleasure of being a thing of the air.

Part VIII
Harley-Davidson

My Life On The Back Of A Harley-Davidson

Once again, late in life, I discovered a new adventure: Motorcycles, especially, Harley-Davidsons.

During all my years in California, I had never ridden a street bike. Along with some of the other guys at Lockheed I had ridden dirt bikes on the grounds of a military base when taking part in a test of the Cheyenne compound helicopter. It was wooded and pretty, with small streams we could ride across. That was my only experience on bikes until one afternoon in Louisiana.

I was driving down Main Street in Pineville, Louisiana when I spotted a small bike for sale. I stopped the car, got out, walked around it, and thought that might be fun to ride. It was a Honda Rebel, styled after a Harley, a good looking little bike. Although it was pretty beat-up, it had captured my interest. Later, I found one just like it in good shape, so I bought it.

Some of my business associates were riders, and they invited me to join them, which I did. They were all Harley riders, but I didn't think anything of it until one day the leader of the group put his hand on my shoulder and said, "Berchman, if you want to keep riding with us, you've got to get a Harley." I was very indignant. What could be so different? Mine looked like a smaller version of their bikes, and I could keep up with them, even though I had to really push it.

In those days, a second-hand Harley was hard to find. It was really a status symbol to own and ride a Harley. One day while driving home from Natchez, Mississippi through the town of Ferriday, I spotted a motorcycle chained to a tree with a FOR SALE sign on it. That can't be a Harley, I thought to myself. But I turned around and went back to take a look at it. It was a Sportster, black and sort of rough looking. I asked the guy, "Does it run?" "Does it run?" he answered. "Listen to this." With that, he cranked up the bike, and I fell in love. It had straight exhaust pipes and roared; suddenly, I understood about Harleys.

Of course I bought it, sold my little Rebel, and became a Harley rider.

That was the start of what was going to become a driving force in my life for quite a few years. I called it my *Adventure Machine*.

Later, I put my name on the waiting list for a new Harley with Johnnie Davis, the local Harley dealer. The waiting list was two years long at that point. However, a little over a year later, Johnnie called me one day and said that a customer was unable to produce the money to purchase a new bike, so he had one available if I wanted it. "The only thing is, it's not the color you wanted." "Johnnie," I said, "I don't care if it's pink, I want that bike!"

So, I became the proud owner of a blue dyna-glide, which I named T-Blue. In south Louisiana, when someone is either a small person or the junior son, they are called *"T"*, like T-Don, or T-boy; it's a term of endearment. My wife, Francy, and I rode that beautiful blue bike down into Mexico and across the U.S.A., from California to Georgia, during two weeks on the road. In addition, we rode to many other destinations around the country and into Canada. We met some wonderful people on that machine and experienced many adventures which would never have happened if we had never ridden a bike. That eventually led me to create a reality TV show called *"Hog Heaven: The TV Show,"* which is covered in another chapter.

With the advent of cell phones, the danger of riding motorcycles increased substantially because the users are not paying attention to their driving. The most common cause of injury accidents involving riders is distracted automobile drivers playing with their cell phones. As a motorcycle rider, you pay dearly for their inattention.

But at the time, like any other thrilling adventure, it was worth it.

The 100th Anniversary Of Harley-Davidson

What a start to this event! As we approached Milwaukee, we were greeted by people waving at us from overpasses as we rode down the freeway. Some even had signs like "Welcome Harley Riders," or "Welcome Home!" These were definitely signs of an up-coming good time. Everywhere we went, we found the locals to be extremely friendly and happy to see us. Events were taking place all over the area.

Riders Ranch, where we were staying, had a full menu of activities scheduled. The House of Harley featured rides around the Milwaukee mile in a NASCAR race car. Thirty miles north of the city was the "Club HOG XX," for Members only. You had to show your membership card to HOG to get in the gate. Then the main event was down on the lakefront where the featured anniversary party was held. If you wanted to party, you had come to the right place. All areas around the lake had an ample supply of vendors of all sorts. The Club HOG featured the Cyber Café, where you could get a free cup of coffee and use their computers to check your e-mail. Each area featured top-name entertainment. In fact, there was so much to do, you could not possibly do it all in one week.

Both the city and HOG had rides set up to enable self-guided tours of the different sections of the state. Francy and I selected a backroads ride which sent us over small, one-and-a-half-lane roads on smooth blacktop, winding through some interesting countryside. At one point, we rode up to a beautiful old church sitting on top of the area's highest hill where you could see for miles around. The view from the upper floor of the church was spectacular, and the interior was beautiful. Back in the parking lot, a priest was blessing some of the bikes, and we asked that he bless our bike also. Funny thing, the ride was a lot smoother after that. Or maybe it was just my imagination.

Anyhow, it didn't matter where you rode, there were bikes everywhere, coming and going, turning left and right, fast and slow. There were stock bikes and beautiful customs, single and two-up, plus many sidecars also. A couple we saw had the side car completely enclosed. Every parking lot at restaurants was packed with Harleys. The local Harley dealers were each putting on their own shows and parties as well. It was estimated there were at least one million or more people there.

Francy and I had the honor of carrying the flag for the Central Louisiana HOG Chapter in the parade. The parade was limited to only 10,000 bikes, so it was pretty exciting to be part of it. The parade consisted of Heroes of the MDA, Harley dealers and executives, at least 1,000 representatives of the HOG Chapters, and lucky folks who had received an invitation to take part.

We had to be at the starting point at 4:00 AM, or as we used to say in the military, O-Dark-Thirty. At 4:30 AM, the group left to travel a short distance to the parking lot of the local zoo where we were issued the poles for the flags. It was interesting to walk around the parking lot, looking at all the Chapters represented. There were members from England, France, Japan, Ireland, Brazil, Germany, Nova Scotia, Canada, Sweden and all the states in the union. We had a nice conversation with a couple from Hawaii, and some folks from New Orleans, Bossier City, Lafayette, and Homer Fugua from Shreveport. When you attend something like this, you realize that as a member of HOG, you are part of something that is truly international in scope.

Soon, other folks participating in the parade began arriving, and they just kept on riding in and riding in, until you felt that all the Harleys in the world must be here for this occasion. It was fun just standing there on the sidewalk, watching them as they rode in.

Finally the call to start was given, and the roar of thousands of Harley engines cranking up filled the air. As we pulled out onto the street, we realized that this was a once-in-a-lifetime experience. The route was seven and a half miles long, and every inch of it was crowded three and four deep with people cheering us on. Francy and I wore our Mardi Gras outfits consisting of Mardi Gras t-shirts for us both, a top hat covered in Mardi Gras beads for me, and a purple wig and cowboy hat for Francy. We received a tremendous reception from the crowds. I got so pumped up that Francy had to calm me down. I was bouncing up and down in the saddle, totally stoked. It was a wonderful experience.

That night was the main event which everyone was anticipating. There was great entertainment, starting with the Doobies; they were great. People were dancing to the music, and excitement was in the air. They were followed by Tim McGraw; the women loved him. The excitement continued with Kid Rock, who stole the show. This guy was great, with lots of energy, and the crowd loved him. Those were our kind of people, the kind of people who loved life and adventure.

But everyone was wondering, who could be the main performer? Everything so far was perfect, the right entertainers for this crowd. Who could be better than this? No one knew, and everyone was guessing, The Stones, Eagles, or ZZ Top. Whoever it was would have to be someone special to follow the groups which had performed so far. Finally, the announcer silenced everyone in anticipation for the main event. *Elton John.* The excitement stopped! This fat little gay guy was in the wrong place. He was NOT a crowd favorite by any means. After all, this was the Anniversary of Harley-Davidson, a macho, American-made machine, and this guy was from England! The crowd began to fade away, and the music died, as the song goes.

However, all in all, it was the only mistake the planners made the entire week. Everything else was first class. I'll never forget the thrill of riding my Harley down the streets and all the people cheering us on. I am so happy that we were able to attend. After all, I don't think we'll get a chance to attend the next 100th anniversary.

The Hog Heaven TV Show

One day while riding our Harleys, my friend, Pete Ferrington, suggested we should find a way to make some money riding these Harleys. How about doing a magazine?

I told Pete, "I have no idea how to do a magazine, but I'll tell you what I do know how to do. "What's that?" he asked. A TV show was my answer. He was hesitant. "A TV show?"

I confidently replied, "Yes, a TV show about riding Harleys; now that is something I know how to do. Don't forget, I have been in the TV business for a few years and have directed a couple of shows, like *"The Louisiana," "High School Rodeo Show,"* and many commercials. In addition, I also know how to get it on the air.

That conversation was the beginning of our adventure in the TV business. We decided we wanted to do a show that portrayed bikers as normal, everyday, hardworking people, and not the outlaw biker type that a lot of people associated with riding motorcycles.

We purchased a TV camera and started planning. The first couple of shows were pretty simple. I found a sky-diving helmet, and we mounted a full sized camera on top of it. We installed an eye piece and an on/off switch so that I could film while riding my bike, with the camera sitting on top of my head. It was pretty crude, but it worked great.

I could ride close-up alongside someone I trusted, like Randy Pate, and actually shoot his speedometer to show we were riding at actual speed. Most shows at this time filmed at slow speeds, then speeded it up in production, but outs was the real thing. This was before the invention of the small cameras used today. I looked pretty weird riding down the highway with a TV camera mounted on top of my helmet.

After getting a couple of sponsors, we bought some time on a local TV station and began airing the show on Sunday mornings. Pretty soon we had developed a pretty good audience, and we decided to expand. I started calling on stations until we were in every market in Louisiana except New Orleans. In addition, we moved onto three stations in Texas, including Houston.

We now had a host, Meisie Pacris, who had worked with me at the TV station. She was very pretty, and the fans loved her. She even got fan mail. Later we added another host, a guy named Jack May who could travel with me. He was a local radio DJ and knew how to interview people and move a show along. He and I traveled up to New Mexico and lower Colorado filming together.

I would contact a Harley dealer in a town we were going to visit, and make arrangements to have some HOG members meet us. After having lunch at their favorite restaurant, I would ask them to take us on their favorite local ride and show us some local scenery. As we rode along the route, we would stop at various scenic spots, and Jack would interview different riders. Some of the common questions were: Why do you ride? What do you do for a living? These kinds of human interest questions showed who these Harley riders were.

The show kept expanding, and we formed a corporation and brought in investors. We were approached by a network in the southeast called Untamed Sports, who wanted to carry our show as well. We were looking good.

One of the major backers we brought in was Stanley Bordelon, who was a member of the local HOG group and a close friend. Another major investor was Wayne Guidry from Opelousas. Wayne was a retired government worker who also hunted alligators. He liked adventure and drove our truck for us on trips. By this time, we had acquired a real camera man, Denis Murdock, who filmed from the back of our pickup truck.

Unfortunately, our host, Jack May, had to leave us to return to England with his wife. As the search for a new host in progress, I happened to watch a parade in which a motorcycle policeman was doing incredible stunts on a Harley. He was good looking and personable as well. His name was Wells Cornette, and he became our new host. He also owned and operated a motorcycle riding school called Top Gun which taught motorcycle policemen how to ride safely. Seemingly by accident, we had found the perfect mix for our TV show. Wells became very popular, and I was often stopped by young girls asking for his autograph while getting gas at a service station. I had to tell them he wasn't with me, and they quickly lost interest when I told them I was the director. Wells and his friend, Chad Guidry, rode with us while filming in the Florida area. I was always searching for interesting, little known subjects to include in the show, and on our Florida trip, we found the country's smallest police station. Of course, Wells and Chad had to investigate, and it turned out to be an old phone booth located in the center of this town. It even sported a sign saying **Police Station**.

Things were going well with our business, when we received an invitation to meet with the past president of Paramount Pictures, who was interested in developing our show. Pete, Stanley and I flew to California for the meeting. When we met him, he had brought along a script writer and a director. We had finally hit the big time. This man wanted to expand the show to one hour, with scripted plots. Up until now, we were one of the first reality shows, unscripted and unrehearsed. We just got on our bikes and rode. We were pretty excited until he started talking money.

He wanted $300,000 up front to do the show, with no guarantees that he could get it on national television. We had a total of $75,000 to offer, with a promise of the balance on the back end. He wanted the entire amount up front, and would not compromise. So, that ended our dreams of a national syndication for Hog Heaven, and we pretty much shut down our operation at that point.

But we had produced 59 episodes, and to this day, we occasionally meet people who say they remember our show, and really enjoyed it. So, we can say we produced a real TV show right here in south Louisiana with a bunch of local businessmen who were learning as they went along.

The Iron Butt Ride

The year is 2004, and it's really dark at 3:15 in the morning, but that's when I had to leave the house to join my friends, Pete Ferrington and Murray Davis at the Texaco station on I-49. We had decided to leave at 4:00 AM in an attempt to complete a 1,000-mile ride on our Harleys in 24 hours. We wanted to qualify as Iron Butt riders by doing a Saddle Sore ride.

The Iron Butt Association is an international organization of long distance bike riders. You don't just get on your bike and start riding. You have to carefully document the entire trip, every stop you make, the mileage, the time, the location, and have witnesses for the start and finish locations. Then you submit to the Association all your information including a map of your entire route with all stops indicated on the map. The Association then verifies your information, checks out the mileage, contacts witnesses, etc. before granting membership.

When Pete and Murray first presented the idea to me, I wondered if I could really do it. After all, that's a lot of saddle time. In the past, I had ridden as much as 400 miles in a day. When my wife, Francy and I rode from coast to coast a few years prior on the Sea to Shining Sea run, we averaged at least 300 miles every day for two weeks. But 1,000 miles in a twenty-four hour period was a whole different ball game. But what the heck? You only live once, and it was a challenge. Besides, I've always considered myself a good rider, a real rider, not a bar hopper, or a show boater, but someone who RIDES. So, it was an opportunity to prove to myself that I could do it.

We were all bundled up in our winter riding gear, leather coat, chaps, long underwear, skull caps under our helmets, scarves and thick riding gloves. Plus a lot of adrenalin. It was dark and cold, but we were excited and eager to begin.

Our first leg from Alexandria, Louisiana to Wascom, Texas wasn't too bad. We rode at a steady speed of 70 mph, which would give us two hours between fuel stops. As we approached Wascom, our first stop, Murry was leading, and Pete was behind me. Just as we pulled off the freeway, I glanced in my rear view mirror to check on Pete, but he wasn't there! Murry and I pulled into the gas station, and looked back toward the freeway and finally spotted Pete on the off ramp. His engine had quit on him, and he had reached down to the fuel switch to get more fuel from the tank, but in the dark, with those big heavy gloves, he couldn't find the switch, and he ran out of gas before he could locate it. All of this happened at 70 mph in the dark somewhere in Texas with traffic all around him.

So began our Iron Butt ride. This was the entry level ride to qualify for membership, and we were not off to a great start. But Pete recovered; we fueled up, got our receipts with the date and time on them, grabbed a bite, and resumed our ride. This time, I was in the lead, followed by Pete, with Murray riding trail. We rotated at every stop so each of us spent time in the lead.

Exactly 137 miles later, Pete's engine quit again. At this point he was leading, in the fast lane of traffic. I was right behind him and before I could react, I was alongside of him, with Murry pulling up as we looked for a place to pull off. We now had to change our plans to accommodate Pete's thirsty engine. That second leg was the worst, as it had gotten colder, and I was shivering. I wondered to myself, "Man, I don't know if I can do this or not." What started off as a lark was now getting serious. The information the Association gives you recommends you don't ride too fast, as it wears you out sooner due to the concentration required, the wind beating you up, and the extra fuel stops required. A member told us that we would hit a wall around 700-800 miles, and if we could get through that, we would be okay.

Thankfully the sun was making an appearance, and we started to warm up; by the next stop, everything was looking a lot better. The three of us roared down the highway, feeling free as only you can while riding a Harley with good friends.

We rode through the Dallas/Ft. Worth area and continued west past

Abilene to a town called Big Springs, Texas. This would be our turn-around point, a little over 500 miles from Alexandria. We made it there in good time, bought the T-Shirts, took some pictures, and had our arrival and departure times documented by the manager of the dealership. We splashed a little cold water on our faces to freshen up, checked the oil in the bikes, cleaned off a few bugs, and we were off on the second half of our journey.

Feeling great, we ate light on the road, learned to get our fuel stops a little closer together, and kept our speed constant at 70 MPH. We never hit that wall the Association had told us about, and rode on to Bossier City, Louisiana, arriving there around midnight. We checked our mileage, and found we had completed the 1000 required miles for the Saddle Sore 1000. We pulled into an all night dinner to eat and discuss our next move. We felt pretty good, and we decided to take it to the next level, the Bun Burner by riding an additional 500 miles within the next twelve hours.

Riding after midnight was a great time to be riding the freeway. There was very little traffic, and the bikes were purring as we roared toward Ruston. At Ruston, good sense took the place of valor, and we decided to get some sleep since we were ahead of schedule. At 2:30 AM, we checked into a motel, leaving wake up calls for 7:00 AM. By 7:30, we were saddled up and back on the road, heading toward Jackson, Mississippi. We stopped at the Harley dealer there, and continued south to McComb, Mississippi.

By this time we were ready for a good meal, and stopped at the Dinner Bell restaurant in McComb. This is a great restaurant, worthy of a trip. We sat down at a round table with a lazy susan in the center packed with good southern food for our selection. You rotate the lazy susan and select as many dishes as you want. Everyone was real friendly and were fascinated by the ride we were doing. We stayed eating and talking too long, enjoyed ourselves too much, and had to have pictures taken before we finally climbed on our bikes for the last leg.

We rode through Hammond, Louisiana and turned back west for

Lafayette. We arrived at the Cajun Harley Dealership in a total of 23 hours and 23 minutes, not a big margin for the Bun Burner 1,500 miles. We were lucky that we did not run into any traffic jams, which would have delayed our ride. The opposite side of the freeway was slammed shut when an 18-wheeler jack-knifed and backed up the traffic for ten miles. We wasted no time getting our gas and receipt which became our actual arrival time. Then the manager of Cajun signed off on our completion time. That made it official!

Since the first of this year, only 33 riders have qualified for the Iron Butt patch in the entire country. And three of them are from Central Louisiana, riding Harleys.

We were now Iron Butt riders and were awarded the license plates to prove it.

THE TURNAROUND POINT

COMPLETION OF 1500 MILES
IN 23 HOURS & 23 MINUTES

STILL ROLLING AFTER ALL
THOSE HOURS

For additional orders of this book, contact:

Berchman Richard

berchmanr@aol.com

or order online at:

Amazon.com

Made in the USA
Columbia, SC
28 September 2020